Spiritual Discourse

Spiritual Discourse

Learning with an Islamic Master

Frances Trix

upp

University of Pennsylvania Press

Philadelphia

University of Pennsylvania Press
CONDUCT AND COMMUNICATION SERIES
Erving Goffman and Dell Hymes, Founding Editors
Dell Hymes, Gillian Sankoff, and Henry Glassie, General Editors

A listing of the available books in this series appears at the back of this volume.

Frontispiece: A "joust" between two Sufi Babas over who has the greater spiritual power. The one riding on the lion proclaims that he can reach the heart of a person though it be like that of a wild animal. He is bested, however, by the Baba riding on the stone, who thereby proclaims that he can reach the heart though it be dead like a stone. The picture was a gift to the Tekke from the family of Ali Orhan, who came to America early in the twentieth century from Voskop in southeastern Albania. Photo by the author.

Cover: Baba Rexheb. Photo by the author.

Copyright © 1993 by the University of Pennsylvania Press
All rights reserved
Printed in the United States of America

Library of Congress Cataloging-in-Publication Data

Trix, Frances.
    Spiritual discourse: learning with an Islamic master / Frances Trix.
      p.   cm. — (University of Pennsylvania Press conduct and communication series.)
    Includes bibliographical references (p.   ) and index.
    ISBN 0-8122-3165-1
    1. Bektashi.   I. Title.   II. Series.
BP189.7.B4T75   1993
297'.7—dc20   92-32060
                                                                        CIP

For Baba Rexheb
and Other Chanters of Nefes

Contents

Acknowledgments

It is with gratitude and pleasure that I acknowledge people of the Bektashi community, my family, and scholars in Near Eastern Studies and Linguistics, who have given all manner of assistance to this book.

For more than twenty years Bektashis of the Albanian Bektashi Tekke (*Teqeja Bektashiane Shqiptare*) in Michigan have received me with kindness and unfailing hospitality. I especially thank Baba Bajram (now deceased), Dervish Arshi, Zonja Zejnep Çuçi, Zoti Ago Agaj, Zoti Xhevat Kallajxhi (now deceased), Zoti Fadil Duro (now deceased), Shije Shahin of Ann Arbor, Ajnur Rakipi of New York, and Hisnisha Ahmedi of Gostivar, Macedonia. Their insights and friendship have been invaluable. I also acknowledge Bektashis in Michigan, Connecticut, New Jersey, New York, Illinois, Wisconsin, Ontario, Kossovo, Macedonia, and Turkey. Their acceptance of me as Baba's student and their sharing of the life of the community have enriched me beyond the bounds of any study.

I also thank my family for their moral support and trust when the purpose of the time I spent at the tekke, in the Middle East and Balkans, and in study of Turkish, Arabic, and Albanian was not always clear. In particular I thank my father who first accompanied me to the tekke, my mother who valued clear writing over all, and my son who has shared travels and life at the tekke.

Turning to the university, in Near Eastern Studies and in Linguistics I have been singularly fortunate. It is thanks to my early teachers of Turkish—Talat Halman, Hikmet Sebüktekin (of Boğaziçi Üniversitesi), and Sabahat Sansa—that when I met Baba Rexheb we had a common language. But it is James Stewart-Robinson of the University of Michigan who has guided and abided me in my continuing study of Turkish. He has shared most generously his time and expertise, and his character and integrity have in no small way influenced my appreciation of Turkish. I also gratefully acknowledge the influence of George Mendenhall in Biblical Studies and K. Allin Luther in Iranian Civilization, both of the Near Eastern Studies Department of the University of Michigan.

In linguistics I studied under Alton Becker, whose vision of linguistics within a historical context and whose involvement in the art forms of the people whose languages he studies have affected my approach. For his inspiring teaching, his counsel, and his discerning ear I am most grateful. Becker also introduced me to Erving Goffman. My debt to Goffman in analysis of interaction is ongoing and apparent throughout this book. In addition, I thank Bruce Mannheim of the Department of Anthropology at the University of Michigan, who helped me integrate linguistics and anthropology through ethnopoetics. And finally, I thank Dell Hymes, whose most careful reading of two versions of this book has improved it.

I undertook the initial writing of this volume while I was at the University of Michigan, but the rewriting has been done while on the faculty of the Department of Anthropology at Wayne State University. I acknowledge the assistance and support of all my colleagues there, especially Andrea Sankar, Barbara Aswad, and Marietta Baba, as well as the generous support of Wayne State University in publication of this book.

More recently I acknowledge the University of Pennsylvania Press, and in particular the enthusiasm and experience of editor Patricia Smith. Through the Press I have also had the honor and benefit of careful readings by Michael M. J. Fischer and Margaret Mills. Their suggestions, building on their expertise with Islamic discourse, helped me balance the Islamic and linguistic contexts of the study.

Looming behind all these contributions is my debt to Baba Rexheb. The whole book can be seen as an attempt to begin to acknowledge this debt.

Note on Vagaries of Spelling

Choice had to be made in this book from among various spellings of non-English, often Islamic words. These words traveled from Arabic contexts through Persian and Turkish ones before finding their way to the Balkans. Along the way pronunciations varied, particularly in the vowels although not confined to them. Thus Baba's name is "Rajab" in Arabic, "Recep" in Turkish, and "Rexheb" in Albanian. As he is baba of the tekke, I use the form he uses, namely "Rexheb" (pronounced "rejeb"). However, with Baba Bayram, who has since passed away, I use the Turkish spelling because it is more likely to lead readers to correct pronunciation than is the Albanian "Bajram" (pronounced "bayram").

In contrast, for the term for "spiritual guide" I use a transliteration of the Arabic, namely *murshid*. Here the Turkish would be *mürşid*, while the Albanian would be *udhërrëfenjës* or *udhëheqës*, which my secular Albanian dictionary translates as "air-traffic controller." I also standardize reference to the student as *talib*.

In most other cases I have chosen the modern Turkish spelling, as the Bektashis are historically an Anatolian Sufi Order and most literature on them refers to this Turkish context rather than the more recent Albanian one. Thus I refer to the Bektashi center as the *tekke,* although in Albanian it would be *teqe*.

Prologue

in which the frustration of a student after many years of study discreetly erupts

"Baba, how did Selim Baba teach you?" In isolation an innocent enough question.

There I sat on my folding chair in the study room of Baba's *tekke*—a sort of "Muslim monastery."[1] And there across from me sat Baba, the then eighty-four-year-old Muslim "monk" who was the head of the tekke.

The room we were in had probably been the dining room of a Michigan farmhouse that in the 1950s had been bought by a group of Albanian Muslims and converted into a Bektashi tekke. Were the former owners to return, no doubt they would have had difficulty recognizing their farmhouse, due to both additions to the building and changes in interior decor and use.

On one side of Baba's chair, where perhaps a tall cabinet of the farm's finest china had once stood, there was now a bed whose headboard and footboard were covered with prayer rugs. Pillows were propped on the bed against the wall. And people would sit on the bed with their legs folded under them, much as they had sat on carpet-covered floors in the traditional guest rooms back in the Balkans.

On the other side of Baba's chair, and under the window, where the dining-room table had once stood, there was still a table, only it was piled high with books and papers. There was a six-volume set of encyclopedias, published in Constantinople in 1901 and written in the Arabic letters of the Turkish of that time. Scattered among the volumes were copies of *Dielli* ("The Sun"), an Albanian-American newspaper, as well as letters to Baba from Bektashis from all over the world. Toward the back of the table were several Qur'ans, along with the sixteenth-century commentary on the Qur'an by Husein Vaiz, and a nineteenth-century defense of Bektashism,[2] the particular Sufi Order to which Baba belonged. And then of course there were the books of poetry. These were in Turkish and Persian by poets like Nesimi (fourteenth to fifteenth century), Fuzuli (sixteenth century), Pir Sultan Abdal (sixteenth century), and Niyazi Misri (seventeenth century). Besides books of collected works of individual poets, there were several anthologies of Turkish mystic poetry written in the Roman letters that have been used in Turkey since the 1920s. The anthologies had been sent as gifts from Bektashis in Turkey and were easier for me to follow. As for Baba, he reads Arabic, Persian, Turkish, Greek, Albanian, and Italian, and so is at home in several scripts; but he prefers the Turkish poetry in its original Arabic letters.

The walls at least had not changed in the tekke study room. They still had the stucco finish that had been such a popular embellishment of American home architecture in the twenties. But on the walls, where once perhaps a mirror and a placid landscape had hung, there was now a lunar calendar, with a small watercolor of Baba's native Albania obscuring half the calendar. Across from that hung a framed piece of Arabic calligraphy— a scarlet background with gold lettering of the first line of the Qur'an: "In the Name of God the Merciful, the Mercy-giving." Over the bed was a photograph of dry and dusty buildings that I was told were the shrine of Ali in Najaf, Iraq—hardly an inducement to pilgrimage. Behind Baba's chair was a large picture of mountains being scaled by two large rams with antlers, reminiscent of the sheep in Albania. No one was sure who had donated it—the tekke has been furnished with gifts, which accounted for the unusual assemblage—but I suspected some Albanian Bektashis who had gone to Alaska and who regularly sent Baba gifts including blankets depicting the midnight sun.

In stark contrast to all this is Baba's bedroom, where the only picture on the wall is a photograph of Selim Baba, Baba's spiritual teacher.

Also in contrast to the study room is the private ceremonial room of the tekke. This large room was the Bektashis' first addition to the farmhouse. The room is carpeted and without furniture. Its pale blue-washed walls are bare. All attention is thus focused on the *mihrab* or "prayer niche" where Baba sits, and on the steps of candles to his right.

Back in the study room, Baba's high-back chair also has the place of prominence. And as we talked, Baba sat comfortably in his chair with one leg curled under him. His baggy pants seem made for sitting like that, but it is his flexibility that makes such sitting possible. No doubt the Muslim way of prayer, in which one kneels and then bows until the forehead touches the floor, facilitates such flexibility late in life. But it is the flexibility of Baba's talk that I would explore and the subtlety of the way he teaches.

When I asked Baba the question about how Selim Baba had taught him, I had been coming to the tekke for lessons, on a weekly basis, for twelve years. One would think that by then I would have known how my teacher had been taught. But I was not even sure, after all those years, how Baba taught me. There was no syllabus. Baba did not announce topics or even initiate talk. Instead it fell into my lap to begin lessons.

I found that initiating topics myself was uncomfortable, for clearly Baba had the greater authority. Baba is head of the tekke. When people come to the tekke they always go first to greet him. This involves taking his hand, kissing the back of it, and putting it to their foreheads. Or if they are "inner members,"[3] they kiss the inside of Baba's hand and then kiss his heart as well. When people leave a room where he is, they back out, bowing in respect.

Behind these gestures is respect and love for Baba as one who took vows of dervishhood and vows of celibacy[4] at age twenty-one, and who has since dedicated his life to serving God and his community. I am an American student from Michigan. How should I deign to initiate lessons?

And yet we have studied together all these years. But what have I learned? That too is problematic. The best answer I can give is that I have learned to come back. In other words, I have been learning a relationship. I have been learning how to be a *talib* (seeker) as the student of a *murshid* (spiritual guide) is known. This is no small undertaking, for the relationship of talib to murshid is a model of the relationship of human being to God. How is this relationship learned? That is the central question of this study, and my approach is to assume that a description of our lessons will shed some light on this issue.

Most of our lessons have been spent talking with each other and reading Turkish *nefes* together. Nefes are the spiritual poems of the Bektashis. After all these years of study together, I should be able to follow these nefes, or at least Baba's explanations. Or, and perhaps this is the most important, if I do not follow I should be patient and trust that what is confusing will straighten out in time. Alas, this is not always so.

In fact, when I asked Baba how he had been taught by Selim Baba, it was precisely in the context of my own perplexity as a talib. Baba had explained a quatrain, I had been confused, I had asked for repeated explanation, and had been even more confused. After a third unsuccessful try, I had cried out in frustration, "Baba, how did Selim Baba teach you?" (In asking this I had hoped to discover how Baba had learned from his own murshid, and by extension what I was doing wrong.)

Baba answered my intent. That is, instead of answering how he had been taught, he answered how he had learned. Baba responded in the Turkish[5] that was our common language.

```
Baba: işte duyarken
FT:                 duyarken?
Baba:                       yaa\
FT:                             {laughs}

        * * * * *

        Baba: thus by listening
FT:                       by listening?
Baba:                             yaa\
FT:                                   {laughs}
```

Baba then went on to respond to my impatience and frustration with myself for not being able to follow the explanation of the nefes.

```
Baba: senin gibi~
      ne kadar~
      ... e- çok şeyler öğrenmişsin sen benden~
                                        {softly}
FT:                                     evet
Baba: ama nasıl öğrenmişsin
      duyarken
FT:           eh doğru
Baba:                   ben sohbet ederim~
      konuşolurum~
FT:             evet
Baba:               sen duyarsin
      hatırında kalkar

        * * * * *

Baba: like you
      so much~
      ... e- many things you have learned from me~
                                          {softly}
FT:                                       yes
```

Baba: but how have you learned~
  by listening
FT: true
Baba: I talk as a friend~
  I speak~
FT: yes
Baba: as for you~ you listen\
  it stands out in your memory

Baba's kindness in suggesting I had learned much from him was salve to my dignity. He did not bother to confront me with the foolishness of my insistence on immediate understanding.

But all was not dismal. The very way I had expressed my frustration and called for help did show I had learned how to ask in a Bektashi frame. For, in asking how Baba's murshid had taught him, I had appealed to the basic relationship of the Bektashis.

I. Introduction

Master-Student Relations

in which the topic of master-disciple relations emerges, and an approach to examining this relationship is proposed

In the thirteenth century, with the Mongols pushing at their backs, Haji Bektash along with other Islamicized Turkmen peoples came westward from Khorasan across Iran to Anatolia. In central Anatolia, Haji Bektash drew followers around him, and a Sufi or Islamic mystic order, the Bektashis, was founded in his name. Two centuries later, in the fifteenth century, Sarı Saltık and other babas or Bektashi leaders came westward with Ottoman armies from Anatolia to the Balkans, where they got as far as Albania. There, more tekkes, or Bektashi "monasteries," were established. Five centuries passed. Then, most recently, in the twentieth century, Baba Rexheb had to flee the Communist forces in his native Albania, who saw established religious leaders like himself as enemies of the state. He too came westward, eventually settling in Michigan. In 1954, along with a group of Albanian immigrants, Baba established the First Albanian Bektashi Tekke in America.

I mention this broad sweep of westward movement as a preliminary, a sort of stretching, before settling into a study that is severely limited in geographical space. The physical parameters of this study are in fact two rooms, one above the other, in an old farmhouse on the outskirts of Detroit. The upper room was amply described in the Prologue. It is there that lessons with Baba have taken place, and where I continue to study with him. The other room, beneath, is the basement kitchen, where daily meals are cooked and served and where people drink coffee less formally, talk interminably, and Baba presides most comfortably at the head of the long table.

Behind Baba's place in the basement kitchen is the squat, black twelve-burner stove whose heat warms the classroom above. Toward the end of the morning lessons, the smells of the midday meal waft upward as well. In the same way, the talk around the meal table, the prayers at the table after meals, and the chanting that occurs spontaneously there all help contextualize the private dialogues with Baba and our reading of mystic poetry that take place upstairs.

Returning to the geographical sweep mentioned earlier, from Khorasan to Anatolia, on to Albania, and from there to America, I would like to note that this process took place over seven hundred years. I mention this time period as background, but also in contrast to the time frame of the present work, whose questions arise from fifteen years of study with Baba Rexheb, whose texts come from the last two years of lessons, and whose particular focus is a lesson that lasted seventy minutes. And although seventy minutes is far from seven hundred years, references and patterns of behavior in the lessons can range back to times even before the founding of Bektashi tekkes in the thirteenth century.

Only here, after presenting the spatial and temporal frames of Bektashism and of the immediate study, I pause. Baba Rexheb would not have introduced things in this way. Instead, when asked about Haji Bektash's coming to Anatolia, the Bektashis' entry to Albania, and his own coming to America, Baba responded in a different manner. In the summaries of Baba's accounts that follow, note the overriding importance of the *murshid*, that is, "the master," "the spiritual guide," or roughly, "the teacher."

First, regarding Haji Bektash's coming to Anatolia, Baba recounted that Haji Bektash Veli was born in Nishapur (Iran). His murshid was Lokman Perende, whose murshid was Ahmet Yesevî. In a dream, Ahmet Yesevî saw a sign that Bektash should go to Rum (Anatolia), and so, following the words of his murshid's murshid, he set out first for Mecca and then to the shrine of Ali in Najaf (Iraq), thus receiving the title of *haji*, "one who has made the pilgrimage." After visiting tombs of many saints, Haji Bektash Veli settled in Anatolia where the first Bektashi tekke was opened. In his lifetime he initiated three hundred *halife*s (a high Bektashi clerical position).[1]

Second, in describing the coming of Bektashism to Albania, Baba recounted that Sarı Saltık, a halife of Haji Bektash, was sent to Rumeli (the European part of Ottoman lands), where he founded several tekkes. Before Sarı Saltık's death in Kruje, Albania, people came to him requesting that he be buried by their tekke or on their lands. Sarı Saltık ordered seven wooden coffins be brought to him. After he died each person looked under the cloth of a different coffin and saw him there, and so Sarı Saltık is understood to be buried in seven places in Rumeli, including one in Greece.

Finally, as for Baba's own coming to America, Baba described it in terms of his leave-taking of his murshid, Selim Baba. Baba did not know that he would never see his murshid again alive, or that he would never return to Albania. He therefore did not carry Selim Baba's poems out of Albania with him. The greatest regret of his life is that he did not bring his murshid's poems to have them published here. But he could not have known that he would not see his murshid again alive, and even had he known, as he noted with sadness, he still could not have asked for the poems.[2] This was Baba's account of his departure from Albania.

Regarding the establishment of a Bektashi tekke in America, after Baba and I walked around the recently built white stone *türbe* (mausoleum) on tekke grounds, where Baba will be buried when he dies, we stopped and stood gazing at the tekke that has grown so in the more than thirty years since its founding. I asked Baba whether his murshid wouldn't have been proud of all his work in America. Baba immediately responded in Turkish, and with utter unselfconsciousness:

Ama hepsi onun nimetinden

* * * * *

But it is all from his blessing.

Thus, Baba's accounts of the westward spread of Bektashism contrast with my earlier accounts of the same phenomenon. Whereas my accounts were dotted with temporal and geographical guideposts, the reference points in Baba's accounts tend to be murshids and their words. Haji Bektash's, Sarı Saltık's, and Baba Rexheb's legitimacy and identity are presented in terms of their relationship with their murshids. In the last passage, the one about Baba's reflection on the tekke in America, it is true that the question was framed in terms of Baba's murshid, but the response further underscores the importance of this relationship.

In the Bektashi world of discourse, that is, in parables and narratives, poetry and prayers, in the rituals and in talk at the tekke, the centrality of the relationship with the murshid, as exemplified in Baba's accounts above, is the norm. The very arrangement at the kitchen table, with Baba always at the head, reflects this, for Baba is a murshid. His disciples or students, who are traditionally known as *talib* (a word derived from the Arabic meaning "one who seeks, who strives after"), are seated to either side down the table. But then Baba is also a talib, for each murshid is a talib of his own murshid.

Indeed, there is an unbroken chain of talibs and murshids through which Bektashis connect themselves to their *Pir*, their "patron saint," Haji Bektash Veli. This chain continues from Haji Bektash back to Ali, whose murshid was the Prophet Muhammad, whose murshid was the Angel Gabriel,[3] and thus to God. One way this understanding is expressed is in *devriye*, or "cycle poems." In these poems, the presence of Haji Bektash is described at the initial creation of the world, with the prophets, with the imams,[4] up into the ritual conducted by a living murshid in the private ceremonial room of a Bektashi tekke.

Building on this continuity, Bektashis come into relation with God through devotion and obedience to their personal murshid. This is expressed in their characteristic poetic form, the *nefes*, or "breath of spirit," of which the cycle poems are only one sort. Nefes are most commonly chanted around a meal table after a ritual in the ceremonial room. In nefes the feelings and devotion toward one's particular murshid are endlessly evoked and elaborated. The nefes can thus be seen as a particular Bektashi language of the murshid-talib relationship. As such, they should shed some light on the relationship. However these nefes readily escape those of us new to Bektashism. Their coherence is not narrative in a Western sense, rather it is a much more subtle linking and contrasting of centuries-old Persified Islamic poetic motifs and forms.

For example, the following text is my close translation of a Turkish nefes by Pir Sultan Abdal (sixteenth century) that Baba particularly likes. I include the first quatrain in Turkish (the full Turkish text is in Appendix B).

> Derdim çoktur kangisına yanayim   hu
>   Yine tazelendi yürek yaresi
> Ben bu derde kande derman bulayim   hu
>   Meğer Şah elinden ola çaresi   hu

* * * * *

> So many are my sufferings, which shall consume me   hu
>   The wounds of my heart again are raw.
> For my sufferings, where shall I find remedy,   hu
>   If there be cure only from the hand of the Shah.   hu

All her garments are finer than the rose.
  Do not scorn the nightingale; it is unfitting of the rose.
Such longing have I endured, my heart is bruised.
  Easily come the fragments of my soul.   hu

My tall and graceful cypress, my plane tree.
  A fire strikes my heart; I blaze.
Toward you I pray, I turn always facing you.
  My prayer niche is between your two brows.   hu

Love is not fulfilled with glances,
  Who flees from love is not a man.
The candle is not put out by the breath of a denier,
  Once afire, the light of passion burns.   hu

I am Pir Sultan, so much you have let yourself fall.
  Without greeting, you come and you pass by.
Why do you flee this loving affection?
  Is this to be the emblem of our way?   hu

If this is the Bektashi language of the murshid-talib relationship, it is an "in-house" language. Much contextualization is needed for it to become meaningful for talibs, not to mention non-Bektashis. In my experience, attaining even some understanding takes years.

For example, the word "hu" at the very end of the nefes and at the end of lines was familiar to me from meal-time in the kitchen. Baba always prayed after meals. When he finished the prayer, he always put his right hand on his heart, bowed his head even lower, and intoned "huu."

For years I assumed that this "hu" was a sort of "amen." And although there were occasional intimations that it meant something slightly different (when I studied Arabic, I recognized "hu" as a way of saying هُوَ , the Arabic third-person singular pronoun "he"); my overriding experience of its usage in closing a prayer kept "hu" akin to "amen" in my mind.

Then after years of study with Baba, I went to Turkey for a summer and returned with some Bektashi books that Baba had requested. As I began to read them to him, I noticed the first page of a book attributed to the thirteenth-century founder, Haji Bektash Veli, began with "hu." "Hu" suddenly showed up all over. That same day I noticed that letters from

Bektashis in Turkey sent to Baba also all began with "hu." Baba's nefes that he had written before coming to America began with "hu." These "hu"s had always been there, but I had been blind to them. It was as if my eyes were suddenly opened.

I began to understand that "hu" was not just a sort of "amen"—a request to God that "thus may it be." Rather, "hu" was like the orthodox Muslim *bismillah* (in the Name of God) that begins each chapter of the Qur'an, and that is recited by many Muslims before engaging in all manner of activities.

"Hu" is similar to "bismillah," not just in usage but also in reference. It is one of the ways that God is referred to in the Qur'an ("He"), and is therefore a "Name" of God. But with the intersubjectivity of pronouns, that is, with the special ability of pronouns to reference immediate participants or contexts of discourse, "hu" (a special "he"), when intoned by Baba, also invoked his own murshid. For in Bektashism it is through the intercession of one's murshid that one approaches God.

Full contextualization of the nefes by Pir Sultan Abdal is a distant rhetorical goal—beyond this book and this writer at this time. My point in bringing it up here is to give an example of talib-murshid discourse from within the Bektashi world of discourse. Baba, who knows hundreds of these nefes by heart, reads them in four languages (Persian, Turkish, Arabic, and Albanian), and writes them in two (Turkish and Albanian), is a fluent speaker of this language. I am not. This then represents a difference in Baba's and my language repertoires. But the difference is not merely Baba's knowledge of nefes; it is also his knowledge of the context in which they are chanted. A critical change during this study—an attunement at the broadest level—was my growing understanding of the public context of recitation of nefes.

A simpler example of attunement relating to nefes was my dramatic grasping of a wider reference of "hu." When I recognized the broader use and more personal reference of "hu," my language had expanded and come closer to Baba's and that of nefes. This instance of attunement, however, did not drop from the sky. In discussing the motif of sudden illumination of a student by a teacher in Martin Buber's *Hasidic Tales,* Harriet Feinberg (1972) noted:

> The momentary illumination usually depends in fact on a shared reference-system, built up over a period of time. The ability to provide a moment of sudden, deep illumination can indeed at times arise in a brief encounter, but it arises out of participation in a community in which teacher and student

have a close relationship that extends over a period of time, even if the one illuminated is not a member of that community. The spiritual strength built up through these attachments is what the *zaddik* [similar to the murshid] draws on to provide the moment of insight for the newcomer, the seeker.[5]

In the terms of the above citation, then, I will study the process of learning of a murshid-talib relationship by studying growth of a "shared reference-system." The movement of this growth is toward the discourse of nefes. But the place of departure is more plebeian.

The place of departure is the lessons in the study room of the tekke, with me on my folding chair and Baba in his high-back one. The particular lesson I focus on took place on a November morning in 1985 in the twelfth year of study with Baba.

The Lesson

in which the history of taping of lessons is recounted, one lesson is selected, and a stab is made at showing what the lesson is not

This book is centered around one lesson that took place early in November of my twelfth year with Baba. More accurately, I draw from the tape-recording of this lesson along with my recollections of it. But as taping of lessons has not always been a common practice at the tekke, I will first sketch the context of taping before describing why the particular November lesson was selected from among more than eighty taped lessons.

For the first eleven years of study I did not tape-record our lessons. Then in the twelfth year I gradually began to tape them. This taping, however, did not occur because of any grand ethnomethodological design. I first brought a tape-recorder to the tekke to record the chanting of laments for particular public ceremonies. One day in April of that year, when we had finished with a lament and the tape-recorder was openly running, I asked what I mistakenly saw as a simple question, "Baba, where does your name come from?"

Now, I was not totally ignorant; in various earlier lessons I had learned that Baba had been prayed for before his birth, and named in a chronogram[6] by his murshid's murshid then. But what I learned from Baba's response to my question on the origin of his name, besides an integration of what I had earlier heard, was that Baba understood his naming as a designation of his duty in the world.[7] I also learned that Baba was willing to continue talking with the recorder on. The very richness of Baba's response and his acceptance of the recorder then led to an increase in taping and a gradual shift in what I taped.

The following week I taped Baba reading several nefes by Nesimi (fifteenth century) and Baki's famous lament on the death of Sultan Suleyman (1566), but I also taped our discussion about meter in these poems. The next week I taped Baba reciting a liturgical poem on the birth of Ali, for it was the week of *Nevruz*, a solar-based holiday[8] that combines a celebration of spring and the Persian New Year with the birth of Ali. But I also taped our discussion of the poem and the holiday.

Thus I shifted from occasionally taping set-off prayers and laments to recording the more overtly interactive discussions of our lessons. This is an important change. Had I stayed with the set-off single-speaker texts, this book might have been a more limited dialect or translation study, more in line with linguistic studies in the first half of this century. Instead, in terms of older linguistic studies, I take what was often the dedication (for how many linguists like Bloomfield and Sapir dedicated their studies to their remarkable informants) and focus on the interactive learning implied in these dedications.

Such scenes of learning, as in the discussions between Baba and me, are much less predictable and less individually controlled interactions than are monologic recitations. I would emphasize the difficulty of individual control of an interaction in which there are multiple parties, especially for readers who are made uneasy by a study in which the interpreter was an overt participant.

Interpreter-participation is common in close analyses of speech interaction.[9] Indeed, understanding of such speech situations requires close interpreter interaction with the participants. However, such interaction does not imply control of the situation. On the contrary, a common reaction of participant-interpreters to hearing the tape of their interaction is reflected in the title of a sociolinguist's paper: "Do I Really Sound Like That?" (Jahr in Trudgill, 1986), and in a sociologist's comment on listening to a tape including himself, "I found myself wondering what he (Grimshaw) would do next" (Grimshaw, 1982).

Taping of Baba's discourse has since ceased.[10] But that leaves a two-year corpus of tapes of lessons from which to choose. After much listening and transcribing of tapes from different times over the two-year period, I selected the early November lesson from the first six months of the taping period.

I was drawn to this particular lesson for its variety of forms of interaction. In terms of Baba's speech, the lesson is rich in narratives, anecdotes, adages, and poetry. And it is from one especially memorable narrative early in the lesson that I draw a name for the whole lesson. Thus, instead of referring to the lesson as "an early November lesson," from now on I refer to it as "the Hizir lesson." (Hizir, a prototypical murshid sometimes associated with Elijah or Elias, figures prominently in Baba's narrative. He also figures in a related narrative in the Qur'an, and is known in the commentaries in the Arabic form of his name as "Khidr.")

Besides variation in Baba's rhetorical forms in the Hizir lesson, there is also much variation in my verbal contributions to the interaction. This contrasts with many other lessons, in which the convention is for Baba to do the lion's share of the talking. As he implied when asked how his murshid taught, it is for me to listen. In particular, in these other lessons I somehow initiate talk at the outset, occasionally read aloud from collections of nefes,[11] listen, show that I am listening, and then help with closure. Baba does the rest of the talking. During such lessons there may be a variety of interaction going on, but because my response is generally silence, oral reading, or forms of "um-hmm," this variety is difficult to investigate with a tape recorder.

In contrast, in the Hizir lesson I make more frequent and varied comments throughout the lesson. One of the results is that instances of misunderstanding and confusion are more apparent. This less "smooth" interaction has the advantage of putting in relief our relationship as seen in our interactive strategies.[12] This is not to say that our relationship is atypical in this lesson; merely that it is more aurally accessible.

A second feature that drew me to the Hizir lesson, besides the variety of verbally expressed interaction, was its overt "meta" dimension. In that lesson Baba and I discussed the relationship of murshid and talib and referred directly to our own relationship. Now all interactions have a "meta" dimension, for, no matter what participants are doing, they are also indirectly commenting on their relationship with each other. But that week, I had just begun to consider writing a dissertation on the relationship of murshid and talib, and my enthusiasm spilled into the lesson in the form of questions on the relationship. Further, my more obvious confusions and vulnerabilities in this lesson led to strategies of mediation on both our parts that put our relationship in yet greater relief.

Finally, besides variety of verbal interplay and explicit references to our relationship, I chose the Hizir lesson for its length. It is seventy minutes long, making it the longest of the uninterrupted taped lessons (here I discount lessons where either Baba or I read aloud extensively from books). This length allows for greater possibility of repetition of patterns of interaction, and therefore, hopefully, my perception of these patterns.

Yet the very length of the interaction that offers such a broad arena for trying out hypotheses of interaction is also a linguist's nightmare. So much can be communicated in a single pause, particularly by those who know each other well. What then of seventy minutes of interaction?

Many linguists and sociologists of language have therefore wisely stuck to analysis of much shorter forms, like a proverb (Becker, 1984); or much shorter periods of interaction: from five seconds (Schegloff, 1968)[13] to five minutes (Pittinger, Hockett and Danehy, 1960) to nine minutes combined (Scollon, 1976) to fifteen minutes (Labov and Fanshel, 1977). The exception is Tannen, who braved over two hours of interaction among six participants (1984).

After transcription, the immediate problem with a seventy-minute interaction is segmentation so that one can reflect on the interaction. Another problem is the rhetorical one of presenting so much interaction for readers. The organization of this book reflects a pendulum-like response to the need for both segmentation and integration in a meaningful frame.

Before leaving discussion of why the Hizir lesson was selected as a basis of study, I return to the point I made earlier of my relatively more varied and more frequent verbal contributions during this particular lesson. A reasonable question is why this greater verbal contribution on my part occurred during the Hizir lesson. A partial explanation was given when I noted that the week of that lesson I had just decided to write on the murshid and talib relationship and so had questions for an outside audience. Along with this, though, there is another circumstance that I see as having influenced the Hizir lesson.

Periodically, people come and interview Baba, for scholarly articles, for radio programs, or just for their own interest in religion. Around the time of the Hizir lesson, a visiting professor had come and stayed at the tekke and interviewed Baba. (As I was wont to do at that time, I taped the interview.) I see the Hizir lesson that took place three days later as a sort of replaying of the professor's interview in which our more usual sort of interaction was temporarily modified. Thus, as a first pass at describing the Hizir lesson, I will now briefly describe the interview that preceded it, both as an event that I feel influenced the Hizir lesson and as a useful sort of foil to my lessons.

Abstractly, the interview had features in common with Baba's and my lessons. Both were interactions wherein one of less knowledge questions one of greater knowledge. In an interview the purpose is presentation to an outside audience. With our lessons this was not usually the purpose, but my idea of writing about the murshid-talib relationship temporarily constituted such an outside purpose. However, there the similarities ended.

In the interview by the visiting professor,[14] the professor's first question concerned the survival of the Bektashi Order. This is a most precipitous beginning, because with no clear successor to Baba, survival even of the Michigan tekke is a pressing question. In contrast, in my lesson with Baba the same week, this question of survival of the Bektashi tekkes also came up, but not so bluntly and not until fifteen minutes into the lesson, and then again at the end of our seventy-minute lesson.

Baba's response to the interviewer's initial question of survival of his Order was defensive, as were his responses to the subsequent two questions on what Bektashism had to offer the world. Baba became less defensive as he started into a discussion of humans as God's *vekil* or "representatives," but he was halted when the interviewer interrupted to ask whether it made a difference how many Bektashis there were.[15]

This sort of shift, from what would have developed into a fuller discussion during a lesson (on the role of humans as *vekil* of God), back to the more distancing question of numbers, occurred frequently in the interview. Here the interviewer's syllabus was showing.

Further, there are instances in the interview where Baba closes a discussion but the interviewer does not acknowledge the closure and merely flies on to another unrelated question. Nor does the interviewer appear to pick up on Baba's signals of irritation. Progressively, Baba's responses get shorter and shorter. In contrast, in the lessons including the Hizir lesson, closure of discussion is negotiated and accomplished together. Comments and references build on immediately preceding discussion, on references earlier in a lesson, and on earlier lessons. This building on preceding talk is described in detail, with examples, in the following chapter.

To give an overall view of the differences between the interview and the Hizir lesson, the interview can be divided into fifteen episodes according to change in topic. These include forty-six questions by the professor over a period of twenty minutes. The Hizir lesson, too, can be segmented into fifteen episodes. These include forty questions by me, but over a period of seventy minutes. In other words, the interview is choppier by number of questions and by shortness of episode. Were the interview like the lesson with regard to frequency of questioning over time, there would be only eleven questions rather than forty-six. Moreover the Hizir lesson itself was an unusual lesson for the variety and frequency of my comments.

The interview finally ended with Baba calling for coffee. This can be read as a sign that verbal repair of social relations was no longer possible; it can be seen as a gesture of mediation over the dissolution of the verbal exchange. But what went wrong?

Several features stand out. First, the interviewer did not recognize Baba's signals: signals of closure of discussions, signals of continuing response, and signals of irritation. Second, the interviewer did not seem able to reframe his questions in more discreet ways. Again and again the matter of survival of Bektashis came up bluntly. This lack of reframing is related to the interviewer's inability to read Baba's signals that some sort of reframing was called for. Finally, the interviewer did not appear to build on Baba's words. At times it almost seemed as if the interview were merely protocol, that the interviewer needed only to get through his questions without being affected by Baba's responses. This may have been a result of nervousness, however, for Baba did not smile or give signals of anticipatory acceptance.

These observations are not meant to denigrate the interviewer. His questions were important ones that showed research and concern. However, reading signals and picking up on interactive rhythms across cultures is difficult. Even reading signals and joining into interactive rhythms within cultures with strangers can be difficult. Given this difficulty, a common strategy is to fall back on outer frames, for example, on questions devised prior to the encounter, and on previously established interactive patterns. I mentioned earlier that one of the puzzling aspects of Baba's teaching was his lack of syllabus. But in listening to the interview, I could understand how a syllabus prepared beforehand by the interviewer and adhered to despite the other's responses ultimately stunted Baba's responses.

One could counter this whole analysis by asserting that the role of an interviewer and the role of a student differ in basic ways. If the purpose of the interview is to get answers to specific questions, then this interviewer-controlled format, as long as it does not utterly alienate the person being interviewed, may be efficient. This theory assumes, however, that the interviewer knows best what he or she wants to know.

With a talib, though, such is clearly not the case. To grow in spiritual understanding, it is precisely the larger frame of what he or she needs to know that the student does not have. Baba's teaching, as I will try to show, nurtures the relationship with the talib, but always with a clear sense of who has this knowledge. And as the murshid models the relationship of the talib with God, any sense of the talib being ultimately in charge is preposterous. Rather than depending on a syllabus, then, the talib relies on the murshid during a lesson. Direction and periodicity are negotiated and affirmed within the interaction. This requires much greater trust and much greater attention than if the talib were to rely on an outside syllabus.

Further, what makes the Hizir lesson so interesting in comparison with other lessons is that there I, too, like the professor, have an outside agenda. My initiating point is that I will write a dissertation on the murshid-talib relationship. Clearly, the requirement of writing a dissertation does not come from Baba. Yet by the end of the lesson I am back in the fold of building on our shared interaction, with Baba steering.

This return to our more common way of interacting is attunement on the scale of the lesson. In the previous section, my growth in understanding the meaning of the word "hu" was also described as attunement. There are, in fact, many scales and figures of attunement that Baba's teaching fosters. Before I present other examples of atttunement and an overview of the study, however, the basic notion of attunement warrants discussion.

Language Attunement

> in which "language attunement" is defined, and the relation and debt
> to neighboring notions and teachers is most gratefully acknowledged

The purpose of this book is to make explicit the implicit perspective and experience of a talib. In linguistic terms, the goal is to describe dialogue in a specific situation of learning; in social terms, it is to describe the murshid-talib relationship.

Bektashi understanding of this relationship is that it is an ongoing one through which the talib is guided along the path to spiritual knowledge. In an attempt to respect the dynamic of the relationship, as well as from the conviction that if a relationship exists anywhere, it is in the interaction of its parties, I look to "language attunement" as a focus of describing this evolving relationship.

The gentle term "attunement" is suggested by Alton Becker (1984), who uses it to refer to the necessary process of self-correction recreated in a philologist's reading of a distant text. His understanding of attunement is that it is never attained but is rather an oscillating approximation toward the world of the distant text. Becker draws his term from John Dewey,[16] but the common parallel is with the tuning of musical instruments for jazz—the self-correction of each musician. "Attunement" thus refers to "a diminishing of difference," or positively, "an increasing coordination."

Attunement is alternatively described by David Blum (1986) in his book on the Guarneri Quartet as "a fifth presence," when all members of the quartet are playing as one: "It is as if the music is playing them." This sort of attunement is one that is attained—attunement as a special state.

The attunement that I describe is a combination of these approximations and arrivals. It is a process—a gradual lingual enrichment of Baba and myself toward a new coherence—but it is also a process with occasional ritual coming together. In an attempt to encompass the breadth of this definition, I define "language attunement" as "increasing coordination through *play-full* recollecting of dialogue with another."

By "play-full recollecting" I intend to suggest several senses of "play." First, the recollecting has varied scope, like a rope with some "play" in it—as short and immediate as a preceding phrasal pattern in a conversation, or as long and distant as a shared story from years in the past. Second, at a far end of the spectrum, participants can get so caught up in the activity, in the "play" of the conversation, that they are transformed. Finally, and this holds across the board, in using the term "play-full recollecting" I refer to the engendering or contagious quality of "attunement" in interaction. This partly reflects the common strategy of matching in conversation, such as when one offers a compliment, and another responds with a compliment. Or in Baba's and my case, an utterance toward the language of another occasions a response toward the language of the previous speaker. But the engendering quality of attunement is more than tit-for-tat; it is observed in interactants' ability and proclivity to use experiences of past attunement as grounds for present attunement. With recurrent interaction, attunement becomes a recursive process, ever expanding in reference and subtlety, leading to the creation of a shared language.

Shared language of this sort is celebrated in a Bektashi context in sessions of *muhabbet* in which participants sing nefes back and forth to each other. In a more mundane way, attunement also can be reached periodically in talk between people who have interacted over a long period of time. My particular aim is to describe strategies that facilitate both the periodic attunement and the more far-reaching attunement, for my understanding of the murshid is that he teaches through such strategies.

This notion of language attunement as "increasing coordination through play-full recollecting of dialogue with another" draws from socio-linguistics, hermeneutics, and cybernetics. Related concepts in each of these fields are "linguistic convergence," "appropriation," and "structural coupling." All of these concepts, it should be noted, are concerned with a way of modeling ongoing change.

"Linguistic convergence," understood as the coming together of two languages or two varieties of a language in the speech variation of individuals, is the ground of sociolinguistics. That such variation can be systematically studied is the premise of the approach. Uriel Weinreich's book *Languages in Contact* (1953) and his later article with his students William Labov and Maurice Herzog (1968) established linguistic convergence as a field of formal study. In the preface to Weinreich's book, Andre Martinet noted that in the past, linguists tended to study linguistic divergence rather than linguistic convergence. Emphasis on divergence kept the "structure of a language" as a thing apart and therefore easier to specify in a structuralist mode. Ongoing change—"interference" as Weinreich still called it, reflecting his historical context—was seen as impossible to study because it muddied up the neat structures. The earlier separatist approach to linguistic study also relied heavily on written records, where variation had presumably spread throughout the system. In contrast, the study of linguistic convergence necessitated study of present structures in speech.

Obviously my study of attunement is a study of speech in which I, too, presume that change can be studied. As for the languages or varieties of languages, there are several. Most prominently, Baba and I speak different dialects of Turkish: he a West Rumelian dialect (Nemeth, 1956, 1961; Friedman, 1982), I a generally more standard Istanbul dialect. Over time, however, Baba's and my dialects are becoming more and more like varieties of the same dialect.

Within the study of linguistic convergence, is a subset, labeled "linguistic accommodation" (Giles et al., 1973), that specifically studies change in mutually intelligible varieties of the same dialect. Instead of defining itself in the historic framework of language change, as linguistic convergence generally has, linguistic accommodation is often contextualized in the broader framework of "interactional synchrony." This broader interactional synchrony includes coordination of body movement, eye contact, speech rhythms, and so forth. Although I do not investigate these aspects, except perhaps for speech rhythm, I also see language attunement as part of the more general phenomenon of interactional synchrony.

Despite these broad perspectives, however, the scope of actual studies of linguistic convergence, including linguistic accommodation, has tended to be restricted to phonological and syntactic features of language. The exceptions are several studies of linguistic convergence in a regional or areal framework (for example, Friedman, 1982) or in an areal and ethnographic one (Scollon and Scollon, 1979).

Unlike most studies of linguistic convergence, both the areal and the ethnographic studies referred to above also include rhetorical or "stylistic" features beyond their descriptions of the usual phonologic, morphologic, lexic, and syntactic features. Moreover, in the ethnographic study cited above, the Scollons extend beyond stylistic features to "world view." Specifically, the Scollons studied language at Fort Chipewyan, Alberta. They sought to show how in that setting Chipewyan and English have come to match more closely in form and meaning. They related their findings and the process of linguistic convergence at Fort Chipewyan to what they term a "world view" of the people.

There is an interesting parallel here with Weinreich's work. Just as he and his students Labov and Herzog targeted the problematic notion of the study of language as a study of discrete structures, so the Scollons targeted the notion of speech community. Instead of coherence of the speech community being one of shared "language" in a political sense, the Scollons posit community coherence in terms of a world view that facilitates language convergence of the multiple languages spoken in that town. As with language attunement, the shared world view is both a dynamic and an interpretation of the situation.

In addition to linguistic convergence, a second concept related to language attunement is the hermeneutic notion of Paul Ricoeur known as "appropriation." Ricoeur brings a distinctive breadth of vision to hermeneutics, the study of interpretation. He sees the aim of all hermeneutics as "a struggle against cultural distance and historical alienation." This description is clearly part of the dynamic of Baba's and my relationship. And while we struggle to understand each other and not be caught in our differences of dialect, generation, religion, nationality, gender, occupation, and other contrasting networks too numerous to mention, in terms of the study, these differences are a boon. They make our adjustments and interactions more visible.

Ricoeur's understanding of the power of a text is particularly stimulating. He sees this power as the potential to disclose a world. Therefore, "To understand is not to project oneself into the text; it is to receive an enlarged self from the apprehension of proposed worlds which are the genuine object of interpretation."[17] The Bektashis would see the power of a nefes as an actualization of the relationship with a murshid, for the inspiration to compose a nefes comes from one's own murshid. Thus the nefes testifies to the relationship. The reciting of a nefes is among other things a recreating of the event of inspiration of a talib by his or her murshid. The murshid is the link to earlier saints, to the founder of the Order, to the imams, and back to Husein, Ali, the Prophet Muhammad, the Angel Gabriel, and God. In Ricoeur's terms the "enlarged self" would then include the spiritual realm.

Instead of speaking of "enlarged self," however, Bektashis and other Sufis speak of "loss of self," of "death before dying." These expressions reflect partly the precariousness of trusting into the Unknown, as well as the reframing that can ensue. But these contradictory metaphors should not blind us to the agreement between Ricoeur and the Bektashis that the event of interpretation or spiritual growth is fundamentally one in which one receives but does not control or direct. Ricoeur calls this event of interpretation "appropriation," or "the making one's own what was initially alien." However, the term "appropriation" has the grave disadvantage of implying that the interpreter is in control. Ricoeur acknowledges the problem, and tries to overcome it by describing the actual process of interpretation as a sort of "play" toward the world proposed by the text.

Ricoeur further acknowledges that many of these formulations derive from Hans-Georg Gadamer. Gadamer's basic notion of "understanding" is that it is "an event in which the interpreting subject does not preside." It is a "fusion of horizons"—the historical horizon of the text with the horizon of the interpreter. In this fusion, the horizon of the interpreter is transformed. Gadamer sees the engagement of the reader in this process of understanding a text as "play." As such it is not a reproductive process of author intent, but a productive process that "lives in presentation."

> What is essential to the phenomenon of play is not so much the particular goal it involves but the dynamic back-and-forth movement in which the players are caught up—the movement that itself specifies how the goal will be reached.
>   Thus the game has its own place or space, and its movement and aims are cut off from direct involvement in the world stretching beyond it. The fascination and risk that the player experiences in the game indicate that in the end "all playing is a being played."[18]

My definition of attunement as a process of "play-full recollecting of dialogue with another" is clearly in debt to Gadamer's and Ricoeur's references to the event of interpretation as a sort of "play." Further, the emphasis of both Gadamer and Ricoeur that in understanding one does not project oneself into the text, but rather one receives a projection from the world of the text, ties in with my understanding of the creation of a new coherence or language between Baba and myself. This "nonmerging" also ties in with cybernetic understandings of the preservation of the individual unity of systems despite structural change within them as a result of recurrent interaction.

The third related notion after linguistic convergence and appropriation is "structural coupling," the framework of which is cybernetics. Humberto Maturana and Francisco Varela (1987) define structural coupling as what ensues "whenever there is a history of recurrent interactions leading to the structural congruence between two or more systems."[19] Cybernetics can be described as a science of patterns and systems as opposed to forces and material. One of its strengths is in modeling feedback in the working of a system. This is important in the concept of language attunement, because the recursive aspect of attunement is one of its central features.

Structural coupling is developed by Maturana and Varela in a cosmology of cognition, *The Tree of Knowledge* (1987), wherein they derive human knowledge by beginning with the interaction of cells in the simplest of living beings. Underlying the whole development from cells to social organization is the distinctive quality of living beings, namely that "their organization is such that their only product is themselves." Another way to phrase this idea is that as unities, they produce their own boundaries, and they can relate to other unities only in terms of their own structures. This construct supports the basic sociolinguistic tenet that there is order in language variation. Maturana and Varela would say that as unities we can change only in terms of what structure we bring to an interaction. In terms of interpretation, we can only perceive from the structures of our current perspective.

Change comes when such unities are in recurrent interaction, causing their structures gradually to accommodate to each other. This might be seen as "adaptation," but Maturana and Varela reject the term because it connotes that the environment is the determinant, when in fact it is the structures of the unities that determine responses. Further, over time there occurs what Maturana and Varela call "structural drift." The conventional term here would be "evolution," but again the problem with this term is that it implies a world of the environment instead of worlds constituted by the structural responses of interacting unities. Like structural coupling, language attunement is a recurrent process. And the structural drift of Baba's and my interaction is toward constituting a world of shared experience of nefes.

Thus language attunement as "increasing coordination through playfull recollecting of dialogue with another" is similar to and draws from linguistic convergence, appropriation, and structural coupling. But in this discussion and in the definition, the vague element is what constitutes "dialogue with another." Why not just say "dialogue" and leave it at that? The reason I add "with another" to "dialogue" is that I want to emphasize the *personal* quality of these rememberings. They are not rememberings of dialogues unconnected to the recollector. Rather, the recollector was most often a party in the dialogues he or she recalls, or at the very least, closely linked to one of the parties.

In the case of the Hizir lesson, "dialogue with another" includes most often earlier dialogues with the "immediate other," that is with Baba and myself. But the rememberings of Baba can also include dialogues with Baba's murshid (Selim Baba) who is long dead. Indeed, a point of this book is that the way Baba teaches facilitates both our attunement with our earlier dialogues with each other, as well as Baba's remembering and sharing of his earlier dialogues with his murshid.

And these earlier dialogues include not just the words spoken, but also the context of the words in the interactive situation of speaking. For example, Baba's memories of nefes are entwined with the ritual context at the tekke where he heard them and participated in their chanting. So just as "language" in this book is not to be understood as a set of rules, similarly "memories of dialogues" are not movable impersonal scripts. Instead "language" should be understood here as "a repertoire of games," to use Ludwig Wittgenstein's term, with the remembered dialogues as a specific set of personally shared games, where the sharing and the context also have theological significance.

A difference in Baba's and my repertoires was his richer experience with remembered dialogues of nefes in ritual tekke settings. This is an important point, for my major confusion in understanding the lesson was an undervaluing of the personal linking of nefes, and an overly restrictive categorization of the discourse situation of nefes.

Progression to a fuller understanding of the discourse situation of nefes is the plot and substance of the fifth chapter of this book. Baba's and my interaction described there is an example of attunement, or increasing coordination, on a broad scale. But the earlier chapters also catalogue attunements between Baba and myself. It is to an overview of all these chapters and their particular processes or "figures" of attunement that I now turn.

Maps of the Study

in which the chapters of this study are most fleetingly characterized, "figures" of attunement are sketched, and Haji Bektash comes in riding on a stone

A map or overview of this study should help readers follow the variety of focal lengths with which I examine the Hizir lesson, and the variety of perspectives from which I view the relationship with Baba.

Briefly, in the chapter following this Introduction, I study the lesson and its interactive structures in terms of episodes. The episode is a basic focal length and segmentation. I look at openings and closings of episodes, at patterns within the narrative episodes, and at what I consider the pivot of the lesson. Within this discussion I present one episode in its entirety.

In the following chapter on the nature of interacting with Baba, I take a different approach, and rather than continue with segmentations and progressions, I describe the lesson from the perspective of "keyings" (systematic signaling of how an interaction is to be interpreted) of the participants. This leads to a negative definition of the lesson. In other words, just as earlier in the Introduction I described the lesson as "not an interview," so in the third chapter I draw from Albanian society and describe the lesson as "not a joust." By "joust" I refer to the practice of verbal duel, of challenge and riposte, that is such a source of pleasure in Islamic societies.

Then in the fourth chapter I return to looking at progressions across the lesson. Here I focus less on structural units like the episode and more on cohesive textures and their emergence. And whereas I came up with a plot and coherence to the lesson as a whole in the second chapter, in this chapter I develop appreciation of the cohesion of Baba's teaching and my learning.

In chapter five I am again concerned with keyings or interpretive frames. But whereas earlier I was interested in frames of the participants, here I look for a frame from Islamic society for the whole lesson. I describe my growing interest with *muhabbet*, the ritual setting of the chanting of nefes, and how Baba finally contextualized muhabbet for me in most memorable fashion in the basement kitchen of the tekke.

Finally, in the last chapter I review the figures of attunement described in the study. I also coax out assumptions, the "walls of my mind," that restricted understanding of the Bektashi context of lessons with Baba. The epilogue is a brief Sufi characterization of the relationship of murshid and talib. I know of no better.

Another sort of map of this book is an overview of the various "figures" or particular progressions of attunement. For example, one figure already referred to is the gross change of format across the lesson, from an unusual quasi-interview format to a smoother, more deferential format that is the common sort interaction between Baba and myself.

Figure of Attunement: **Gross Change of Format**

(episodes 1 to 7)
interviewlike
multiple shifts of direction of discussion
reference to project outside lesson (dissertation)

$$\longrightarrow$$

(episodes 8 to 11)
usual interaction of Baba and me
continuous direction of discussion of narrative
total demise of reference to outside project

Another example (second figure) of a figure of attunement is found at the level of episode structure. Here I see the direction of drift toward an interchange of personalized nefes. The vertical axis represents time through the lesson, and the horizontal axis drift toward nefes.

Figure of Attunement: **Drift to Nefes**

reference
    $\longrightarrow$ response
            reference based on interaction
            $\longrightarrow$ response toward Bektashi form
                    nefes
                        $\longrightarrow$ nefes

The second figure thus leads to interactional attunement wherein a nefes calls up in response another nefes. Baba and I did not reach this attunement in the lesson, but that was the direction of our interaction. More humbly, in the episode described in detail in chapter two, we did arrive at a shared concern for the future of the tekke.

Supporting the second figure is the figure of the gradual surfacing of nefes in the Hizir lesson (third figure).

Figure of Attunement: **Gradual Surfacing of Nefes Across the Hizir Lesson**

1st episode:
> at close, my aphoristic statement and Baba's

4th episode:
> at close, my aphoristic statement, nefes by Baba

6th episode:
> nefes behind whole episode

7th episode:
> early in episode nefes by Baba

These figures of attunement and others will be developed in the context of the different chapters. However what is missing in these summary figures, as in summary as a genre, is a shared sense of pleasure. Since I defined language attunement as coming about through "play-full recollecting of dialogue with another," this omission is significant. In an attempt to rectify neglect of the emotional texture of attunement, and with the understanding that a "taste" is also a sort of "map," I offer the following example of attunement in the Hizir lesson. It is necessarily at a much finer level of analysis than episode structure or rhetorical form.

The relevant passage took place fourteen minutes into the seventy-minute Hizir lesson, near the end of the first episode. Baba had just made a distinction between *murshids* (spiritual teachers) and *ustaz* (teachers). I had then asked Baba how one knew if someone was really a murshid, or just a teacher. Baba had explained that in the past, murshids would bring word to their talib through what were "like miracles." Baba continued that thus the talib would know the murshid was a true murshid, "that he saw not just from the front, but from the back as well." I had not heard that expression for what must refer to "special vision," but the picture in my mind of "eyes in the back of the head" made me laugh. Baba laughed too. Then, to check that I understood what "like miracles" referred to, I asked:

FT: hazreti Bektaş- hazreti Bektaş Velinın
       bu taşe~
Baba: **binmesi**
FT: **binmesi**~
       boyle gibi **mirakl?**
Baba: **mirakl** yaa\
       .. **boyle**dır\

       * * * * *

FT: his majesty Bektash- his majesty Bektash Veli's
       on a stone~
Baba: **his riding**
FT: **his riding**
       that sort of **miracle?**
Baba: **miracle** yaa\
       .. **that sort** it is\

I have highlighted the obvious attunement of "tracking," that is, the immediate repetition of words of the other: my tracking of Baba's "his riding," and Baba's tracking of my "miracle" and "that sort." But were I to single out all instances of attunement, the entire passage would be bold-faced. It is this density of attunement that I later use to develop the notion of an "attunement slide."

Beginning at the top of the passage, my reference to (Haji) Bektash Veli's being "on a stone" harkens back to a story Baba has told me on several occasions in previous lessons. Briefly, in that story another spiritual teacher wanted to prove that he was superior to Haji Bektash. So he rode in on a wild animal, showing that he could tame the heart of humans, though it be wild like that of an animal. In response, Haji Bektash proceeded to ride in on a large stone, besting the other by showing that he could restore to life the heart of humans, though it be dead like a stone.

In the room next to the study, there is a picture depicting this story (see frontispiece). Baba had first told me the story in the context of explaining the allegorical picture of two bearded men in ritual headgear, one riding on a strangely docile lion, the other riding proudly on a large flat

stone. Baba's telling of the story had been a sort of translation of the picture for me. Later tellings had come up in other contexts, and because it
was a memorable picture and story, by the second telling it was already
part of my repertoire as well. Thus, in referring to this multiply shared
story, I was recalling our earlier dialogues on the story that themselves
were occasions of attunement.

Baba's response to my minimal evoking of this story (in only five
words) was to show that he had picked up my reference. He did this by
fitting in closely with my immediately preceding language. In particular,
he played into and completed a genitive construction that I had begun. In
Turkish, the genitive is marked on both components of the construction.

veli**nin** binme**si**

* * * * *

veli**'s** riding (**his**)

Baba's providing the second word of my genitive construction shows very
close semantic and syntactic coordination with my language. It demon-
strates his close attention and attunement with my talk.

I follow this coordination by "latching" onto his utterance "his riding." That is, my next utterance, which happens here to be a repetition
but need not be, comes without discernible pause after Baba's utterance.
This close coordination of speech rhythms is a form of attunement as is
the tracking we both engage in in our immediate repetitions of each other's words.

My next word, *boyle*, or "this sort," I pronounce with a back vowel
(*o*), as in Baba's West Rumelian dialect, instead of with a rounded front
vowel (*ö*) as it would be in more Standard Turkish. Ninety percent of the
time I use this common word in the Hizir lesson, however, I pronounce
it the Standard way. My movement here to Baba's dialect of Turkish then
is a tuning to him.

In Baba's next turn, he too uses "boyle" in "boyledir" as a response to
my question and an echo of my words. However, Baba's use of "boyle"
here is more than a response and an echo, for, as we will see in the next
chapter, the most common way Baba signals closure of an episode is with
the phrase "işte boyle" (thus it is so). The enclitic suffix "-dir," reinforced
by the preceding minute-long pause ("mirakl yaa\ .. boyledir\"), combine
to suggest a shift in meaning of "boyle" from "that sort" as I had used it

(that sort of miracle) to "it is so." Thereby Baba signals closure while at the same time playing on my words.

What do all these attunements signify? First, there is pleasure. To refer to a shared story with only five words and a nod of the head toward the next room is to play collusively. That Baba is part of this is clearly seen in his close play into my words. And his completing of my genitive construction is an artistic response to my question of whether that sort of story was indeed the kind of miracle he had been referring to in his distinction of murshid and teacher. My use of his dialect in "boyle" can be understood as a continuing of our play, a refusing to step back. My dialect of Turkísh is generally considered of higher status than Baba's regional one, but to ask a question in a higher-status dialect would send a possible message of superiority that I want no part of. Baba's following reference to a second meaning of "boyle" is a sort of punning.

A second significance of such multiple attunement is that it marks a coming together of Baba and myself near the close of an episode. Episode structure will be discussed in the next chapter, but the point here is that twenty seconds after this passage we had closed the first episode of the Hizir lesson.

A third significance of this passage is that Baba and I have yet another instance of attunement under our belts on the basis of the old Bektashi story. Hearing such stories again and again reinforces patterns in the story. One pattern of this story of the baba on the lion and the baba on the stone is the progression from animal to unliving thing. This is a sort of negative definition of human being. Going the other way, from unliving thing to animal to human, leads to God.

Overall, the attunement slide just described was for Baba and myself a reassurance of a shared past, and a testament to current attention. It is in this soil of trust and attention that the relationship of murshid and talib grows from attunement to attunement.

II. The Interactive Structure of Episodes in a Lesson

The focus of this chapter is internal bracketing of the Hizir lesson. Such bracketing provides grounds for the division of the lesson into parts that can then be analyzed and defined as units. Internal comparison of such units is the basis of a structuralist description, but the establishing of brackets and the defining of units are not just creatures of analysis. In a seventy-minute conversation between people of long-standing companionship, conventions of interaction and a periodicity in the flow of conversation are to be expected. Further, these conventions of interaction are an important form of attunement, for they most certainly if unconsciously reflect recollection of earlier dialogues between Baba and myself.

What then are the episodes of the lesson? How are they bracketed? And what messages do variations in their bracketing carry?

Where the Lesson Breathes

> in which it is shown that topics alone are insufficient for setting off episodes, that bracketing of episodes is better defined through negotiated boundaries, and that it is through these boundaries the lesson under scrutiny breathes

In most studies of conversation, topics are the basis of episoding. Centering on topics, however, may reflect the particular sort of interactions that have been chosen for study. For example, the most common sort of conversational study to date is the interview.[1] The next most common sort appears to be teacher-student interaction in the classroom.[2] In both the interview and the classroom situation, transfer of information or checking up on information is seen as important. This lends itself to topical episoding of the interaction. But even in other sorts of studies, like Deborah Tannen's on conversation around a holiday meal (1984) and Labov and Fanshel's on a psychotherapeutic session (1977), episodes were defined by shift in topic (although Tannen added that sometimes the episodes were also centered around an activity, and Labov noted that the topical segmentation, which he nevertheless used, was at a superficial level of organization).

Related to the choice of interactions, but in a broader frame, is the tendency in western society to think and organize in terms of topics, of nouns, of titles. An illustration of this inclination is the way we index poems. In the West, most poems have titles. These titles, the poet's last name, or the first line of the poem are how we organize for retrieval of poems in our indexes, anthologies, and libraries.

In contrast, the Sufi poems that Baba knows have no titles. They are indexed by the poet's pen name that is worked into the first line of the last or second to the last couplet of the poem. For example, in the nefes by Pir Sultan Abdal translated in the Introduction, the second-to-last couplet begins:

Pir Sultanım kani yüksek uçarsın

In collections of poetry by a single poet, individual poems are indexed alphabetically by the first letter of the rhyming segment that is picked up across the nefes. Again, with reference to the nefes by Pir Sultan Abdal, this letter would be an "a" from the rhyming segment "-aresi":

Yine tazelendi yürek y**aresi**

Poems are presumed to be remembered by couplets, but not necessarily the first one, a method that strikes me as distant from a topical organization. And certainly the way people have been trained to recollect would affect how they teach.

This leads to the point that I do not see topics as the basis of segmentation of the lesson with Baba. Rather, sequences of interaction seem more related to the righting and affirming of our relationship with each other and to progressions of associations. Throughout the chapter I will illustrate how the meaning of an episode is esssentially an affirming of Baba's and my relationship. This should be clearest in the section on vulnerabilities of openings. But here I would prefer to illustrate with two examples what I mean by progressions of associations.

One sort of progression of associations is played out in the first quarter of the Hizir lesson. I began the lesson by initiating talk on the murshid-talib relationship. Baba's first response to this was to recite the adage in Arabic:

> the murshid is to his talib
> as the Prophet to his community

(The "Prophet" here is, of course, the Prophet Muhammad, and the "community" is the community of Muslims. Muhammad's concern for the Islamic community is a theme throughout the Qur'an.)

Sometime later, after two more reframings on my part, Baba made the point that Sunni or "orthodox" Islam saw the relationship of human being to God as a direct one without intermediary. He then repeated the above adage, only this time in Turkish, after which he made the point that Bektashism, in contrast to Sunni Islam, adheres strongly to the belief in intermediaries between humans and God, the murshid being such an intermediary.

With the point of the murshid being an intermediary as frame, Baba then moved into a long narrative on Hizir and Musa. In this narrative, though, the talib (Musa) questioned the actions of the murshid (Hizir) in open disobedience of the murshid. After the narrative, Baba countered the negative actions of the talib in the narrative with the following adage in Arabic:

> the talib should be to the murshid
> as a corpse in the hands of the body-washer

In other words, unlike Musa in the narrative, the talib should be totally submissive and trusting.

Is the topic here murshids and talibs? That is true of the whole encounter. Are there several topics, one of the murshid being like Muhammad, one of the murshid being an intermediary, and one of talibs as totally submissive? Or is this interaction more about how to think and talk about the relationship of murshid and talib in terms of the narrative and the adages that move from a more "Sunni" or "orthodox nonmystic Islamic" referenced adage of the Prophet in response to my first questions, to the decidedly Sufi adage of submission of the talib given after the narrative? I find more coherence in the progression of linkages from the outer inward (Beeman, 1986), that is, from the Sunni to the Sufi in Baba's explanation, than in a topic or topics.

Historically it has been safer to begin with Sunni images as a grounds of legitimacy, because political power in the Ottoman world was overwhelmingly in the hands of the orthodox Muslims. Theologically, though, this is also the starting point of argument, for all legitimacy is grounded in the Qur'an. Sufism or Islamic mysticism then progresses from the outer Sunni form to an inner Sufi meaning, for example, by affirming the importance of the Sunni injunction to pilgrimage but then understanding true pilgrimage not as a physical journey to Mecca but rather as a spiritual journey to the heart. Again, this parallels Baba's progression from the orthodox Sunni simile of the murshid being like the Prophet to the Sufi metaphor of the murshid as body-washer, as intermediary.

During the Hizir lesson, after Baba's adage on submission of the talib, I continued with my assertion that:

without a murshid, one sees nothing

Baba's response to this was to offer similar aphorisms prefaced by "we say," leading into a contrast between spiritual teacher and teacher (murshid and ustaz). As mentioned, this response seems less about a topic and more about a progression toward a Bektashi phrasing and framework.

Yet another sort of sequence that does not fit well with topical organization is a sort of zigzag Baba and I engage in forty minutes into the lesson. There Baba suggests I read more about the line of murshids preceding Haji Bektash, but I say that I prefer learning from him because it sticks better and I like the stories. And furthermore, how did his murshid teach him? (This was not the instance referred to in the Prologue.) Baba responds that his murshid taught with stories, parables, and supernatural tales of the saints, after which he explains the source of such supernatural powers in the "chain of the Order," which I relate to the laying on of hands in the Christian church. Somehow a topic is not interactional enough to categorize such movement.

Thus a topic does not appear to serve as the focus of episodes. This is not to say that a change in topic, like the change in motifs in the nefes, cannot be related to the bracketing of an episode. The constraint is that a change in topic alone is not sufficient as a bracket.

In fact there do appear to be interactive patterns around some places where I bring up a topic not related to immediately preceding propositions, but the patterning starts before I introduce the new topic. For example, about twenty minutes into the lesson the following dialogue transpires in Turkish:

1. Baba: . and whatever you should write you know well\
                                                    {soft voice}
2. FT: yes\
3. Baba: there is materialism as much as one wants\
                                            {soft voice}
4. FT: yes
5. Baba: **thus it is** this way\
6. FT: hnnn
        . **thus** it is good Baba\
7. Baba: yaa
8. FT: .. do you know~
          .. hey let's have a look\
      {checks the tape-recorder}
          as for me what I like are stories\
                                            one thing I like
          -is stories\
9. Baba: yaa
10. FT: for example that one on Hizir and Musa~
          (it shows) ex-
11. Baba: yes
12. FT: -actly a mur-
13. Baba: ex-
14. FT: -shid
          what he is\
          are there others Baba~

The second half of this passage (after line 7) with its hedging,[3] pausing, faltering syntax, distraction toward the tape-recorder, and finally my question (in bold) with its direct reference to Baba all constitute what

I consider the beginning of an episode. But the immediately preceding passage (before line 8) is also patterned in Baba's "işte boyle" (thus it is this way) and my repetition of "işte" in "thus it is good Baba" and softer voice.

In fact, in going through the lesson, I found the discourse marker "işte" to be an important signal of closure. Semantically "thus" has potential for closure. But more important, in our other lessons across the years, Baba has used it to mark the closing of a discussion. For example, one of the earliest lessons taped (July 1985) was on the life of Baba's murshid's murshid (Ali Baba, 1826–1903). After telling of Ali Baba's life, Baba finished his narrative by reciting the couplet in Persian that Ali Baba had composed in his last hours. Then Baba said the following:

> . **işte**~ bu beytten sonra~
> eh- bir kaç sahat yaşadi~
> sonra geçti dunyadan\
> .... **işte**~
> onun tercume-i hali budur\

> * * * * *

> . **thus** after this couplet~
> well- he lived a few hours~
> then he passed from the world\
> .... **thus**~
> this is his life-story\ {archaic phrase}

At that point I asked Baba about the meaning of the couplet he had recited in Persian. After a few more comments, Baba again said: "işte \," and I added, "it's complete Baba\." The taping and lesson ended.

A working hypothesis then is that episodes in the lesson may be bracketed by a cluster of utterances and interactive moves, including most prominently "işte" but also pausing, my introduction of a relatively new topic, hedging, and a direct reference to Baba.

In perusing the lesson, other interactive strategies group with "işte." One of these is Baba's reciting a poetic couplet or line from the Qur'an, glossing it, and then following immediately with an "işte" phrase. Another common co-occurring strategy is laughter from both Baba and me around the "işte" phrase. A summary of these co-occurring bracket markers is shown in the figure.

Figure of Attunement: **Bracket Markers of Episodes**

END of episode
    (quotation)
    (shared laughter) + işte

BEGINNING of episode
    + pause + (hedging) + my introduction of a topic (new or
    continued) + direct address to Baba

Seeking sequences of these sorts, I find ten such brackets delimiting eleven episodes in the lesson. In contrast, with more subjective topical segmentation I identify at least thirty-two major shifts. Certainly eleven units are easier to deal with than thirty-two. But more important, the bracketing with "işte" has the advantage of being constituted by both Baba and myself; these are negotiated boundaries.

The next figure is an overview of the Hizir lesson, segmented by the negotiated boundaries just described. On the left, the first topic of the episode is listed, while on the right are chains of associating or interacting found within the episode.

An Episode Map of the Hizir Lesson

(episode) (no. of minutes)	
(first topic)	*(chain of associating/interacting)*
1. (16 min.)	
relationship of murshid and talib	Sunni ⟶ Sufi
	my words ⟶ Bektashi form
2. (4 min.)	
no murshids in America	my words ⟶ Sufi terms
	concern for Bektashism
	⟶ future of tekke
3. (3 min.)	
good topic?	confusion ⟶ self-correct
4. (8 min.)	
more stories like Hizir and	inappropriate question
Musa	⟶ remedy
	⟶ mediation of remedy

5. (15 min.)
   Bektashism full of murshids   Bektashism —→ other faith
                                        zigzag to chain of the Order

6. (7 min.)
   suggest lessons on great   inspiration as mediation
   murshid   my aphorism —→ nefes

7. (7 min.)
   is music like poetry?   confusion —→ distress
                                       —→ mediation
   ——————————— 4 "işte"s ———————————

8. (3 min.)
   Baba Bayram's life story   word —→ vindication

9. (3 min.)
   how long Baba Bayram at   history —→ purpose of visit
   tekke

10. (3 min.)
    how met Baba Bayram   Egypt —→ America

11. (1 min.)
    when Baba Bayram became a   circumstances —→ purpose
    baba   —→ concern for future of tekke

{telephone rings}
{called to lunch}

What stands out in this map of the Hızır lesson is the change after episode 7. All the episodes after this internal bracket have a unifying reference to Baba Bayram. But the bracket after the seventh episode stood out in my mind before I looked at later episodes. That bracket has the unusual distinction of including four "işte"s. This gave it special prominence among the other brackets which at most include two "işte"s.

Further, not only do the episodes after the bracket of four "işte"s have a unifying reference, but also they can be characterized as a sort of connected narrative in which my contributions can be seen as transitions within the narrative. In contrast, the first group of episodes (1 to 7) has a much greater variety of references, and Baba's and my verbal contributions are less smooth. This first grouping of episodes before the line of four "işte"s is also much longer (sixty minutes) than those after the line of four "işte"s (ten minutes).

The immediate problem is to characterize the interaction of the first group of episodes. If, as it appears, these are more varied, then starting with them should not distort perception of the apparently more uniform pattern of interaction in the second group of episodes.

But before moving on to describing specific episodes, I return to the character of the boundaries that delimit these episodes. As mentioned, the boundaries are negotiated ones. Yet it is Baba who initiates them—either with the finality of his quotation, or with his statement of an "işte" phrase—and I who recognize this closure. That these boundaries include both our contributions shows the extent to which we have become attuned to each other's signals in ordering our talk. Or, seen more differentially, I may initiate a topic, but by earlier initiating closure, it is Baba who has given me the floor.

The Withholding of Affirmation

> in which an entire four-minute episode is presented wherein the negotiation of its closure reveals the expected structure of closure as well as how a most delicate subject was broached

In the last section I put forward preliminary bracket markers of episodes in the Hizir lesson, and thereby segmented the lesson into eleven episodes. Bracket markers of episodes are not just creatures of analysis; they, too, are features of attunement. That is, they testify to Baba's and my many previous dialogues with each other. And, as conventionalized features of attunement, variation in their usage carries messages.

To provide a context for discussion of bracket markers, and at the same time give readers a less interrupted view of Baba's and my interaction, I present a complete text of one of the eleven episodes of the Hizir Lesson. The episode I have selected for such an investment of time and analysis is the second episode of the lesson, beginning seventeen minutes into the seventy-minute whole. The main reason I selected this episode is that the friction in the last half places Baba's and my expectations in clear relief. I also chose this episode because it is relatively short—four minutes or fifty-two turns.

The immediate context of the second episode is the first episode. Indeed, I draw my opening of the second episode from a point Baba had made in the first episode. There I had noted that I did not see a relationship like that of murshid and talib in America. Baba's comment had been that there were no murshids in America. That is, instead of speaking in terms of a relationship, Baba spoke in terms of the murshid. My picking up on Baba's comment thirteen minutes later is an example of attunement across the lesson.

The only other reference that warrants explanation before presentation of the text is the darkened lines. I have marked in bold Baba's "işte" (turn 26), my withholding of affirmation (turns 29 and 31), and at the end, my "işte" (turn 51). These are important in the ensuing analysis.

Otherwise the episode should be clear enough in itself. When reading

Episode 2: Turkish⁴ Transcription

1. FT: .... nasıl baba~
            .. ki~ . ben göriyorum bu eksikliktir\
                                    \Amerikada\
            . ki murşid yok\
2. Baba: yok\ burda\
            oylesin\ ruh-değil Amerikada~
            butun yerlerde şimdi artık\
3. FT: hmmm
4. Baba: yani~ o~
            manevi yoluni tutanlar~
5. FT: evet\
6. Baba: yalnız~
            ah- ruhani adamlardır~
            . ta <ehl-i TARIK>\
            ehl-i tarik~ ne burda var
            ne her yerde var şimdi bo-
            Amerikada da bozuldi~
            şey~ eh~-
            Turkiyada da bozulmişler~
            ve~ Arnavutlukte bozulmiş~
            her yerde boyle\
7. FT: ...... değiştir- değişecek MI baba\
            ne düşünüyorsun?

through it, though, I recommend consciously slowing down. In particular, notice the placement of turns across the page. When the utterance of a turn begins directly below the end of the other speaker's utterance, this indicates that there was no discernible pause—less than a half-second—between turns. (See Appendix A for a guide to conventions of transcription.)

It is also important to remember that the Turkish text, with English translation on the facing page, is a transcription of a tape of spoken interaction. The format was specifically designed to emphasize the flow and coordination of talk: here, across and down the page; there, at the tekke, through the morning.

English Translation

1. FT: .... so Baba~
            .. that~ . I see that they are lacking\
                                                \in America\
            . that there are no murshids\
2. Baba: there are none here\
            such ones\ spirit- not in America~
            in all places now there are no longer\
3. FT: hmmm
4. Baba: that is~ those~
            who hold to spiritual {vs. material} ways~
5. FT: yes\
6. Baba: only~
            ah- they are spiritual {vs. corporeal} persons~
            . or < people of the WAY>\
            people of the way~ they are neither here
            not anywhere now des-
            in America it is destroyed~
            whatever yes~
            in Turkey too they have been destroyed~
            and in Albania destroyed~
            in every place it is this way\
7. FT: ...... will it change- will it change Baba?
            what do you think?

8. Baba: ahh ooo
                    o belli değil\
                    . po~ bir şey var\
                                    \Bektaşilikte~
                    her şey gayip- < hiç bir şey gayip olmaz>\
9. FT: .. hmmmmm
10. Baba: .. her var ise gelecek bir gun~
                    .. gene var\
                                    \olur o\
11. FT: . hmmm
12. Baba: ama ne kadar . zaman ister o~
                    belli değil\
13. FT: . ama [hi-
14. Baba: [be- benz- belkim yuzlerce~ sene~
                    kim bilir\
15. FT: . am- hi- yani . muhim bir şey gayip etmez
                    [de-
16. Baba: [gayip etmez ya\
                    .. her şey- uhh bir fi- filozofi da var\
17. FT: evet\
18. Baba: eh ki diyor ki~
                            < her şey gayip etmez>
                    bilmem kim- hangi filozof
19. FT: [evet
20. Baba: [ki soylemiş buni\
                    ki her şey gayip olmaz\
21. FT: . hmmm
22. Baba: .. bile~
                    . uh naimi-n soylediği
                    . yok mi~
                    kyi~
                        \ .. yok değil Naimi-n
                          var ni- niyazi Misrini-n\
                    .. kyi~
                    .... uh~ diyor kyi~
                    . uh
                                < ..... oğlunun . içinde~
                                . babasi saklanmiş\>

8. Baba: ahhh it
                     it is not clear\
                     . but there is something\
                                       \in Bektashism~
                     everything is hid- <nothing is ever lost>\
9. FT: .. hmmmm
10. Baba: .. whatever there is in a coming day~
                     .. again it is\
                                    \it will be\
11. FT: . hmmm
12. Baba: but how much . time it needs~
                     it is not clear\
13. FT: . but [ne-
14. Baba: [li- like- maybe hundreds of years~
                     who knows\
15. FT: . but- no- that is . important things are not lost
            [it me-
16. Baba: [not lost\
                     .. everything ah and there is a philosopher\
17. FT: yes\
18. Baba: eh who says that~
                              < nothing will be lost>
                     I don't know who- which philosopher
19. FT: [yes
20. Baba: [who said this\
                     that nothing is ever lost\
21. FT: . hmmm
22. Baba: .. and even~
                     . ah Naim has said
                     . isn't it~
                     that~
                          \ .. no not he Naim
                     it was of Niyazi Misri\
                     .. that~
                     .... ah~ he said that~
                     . ah
                              < ..... inside . the son~
                              . the father is hidden\>

uh- pan- pantheisme bakımından~
pantheisme bakımından~
uh bir . uh şey- YOL\
bir . yoldi-r kye diyorse~
        <hiç bir şey gayip olmaz\> ne imiş~
uh .. valit~ {Arabic}
        \. yani peder~ {Persian}
uh mevlude {Arabic}
.. girir\
ama nasıl girir?
yani mevludi olurse~
tabii ki~ bir validın vari-
-vari- var- olmali bunun\

23. FT: haaa
24. Baba: ...   oğlunun içinde~
       .. haaa   {below in Albanian}
           < .. tek i biri jetë i gjati
           kiron sot në këtë jetë\
           është fshehur i ati
           kjo është fjalë e vërtetë\>
       işte bu~
25. FT: olmali ya\   {soft voice}
26. Baba: **işte** ondan cihe- şey eder\
27. FT: \ama manevi [bakımından
28. Baba: [manevi bakımından\
29. FT: . hmm .. **ama daha zor bu günler**~
       çünkü bu şey
       inşallah gayip etmez [fakat
30. Baba: [çok-
31. FT: **belli değil**\
32. Baba: BAKSANA~
       uh şimdi materialism ilerliyor\
33. FT: . hmmmm
34. Baba: . ne kadar iler -lerse materialism~
       . mavevi~ . uh duşur\
       am- gayip olur duşur ama~
       uh duşur\
       gorunmez ama~
       gayip olmaz\

ah- pan- from the view of pantheism~
from the view of pantheism~
ah one . a whatever- WAY\
it is a way of which is said~
        < nothing will ever be lost\> which is~
ah .. the father~ {Arabic}
        \ . that is the father {Persian}
ah to his child {Arabic}
.. he enters\
but how does he enter?
that is if there is a child~
of course~ there is a father-
there is- there- must be one\

23. FT: haaa

24. Baba: ... inside the son~
     .. haaa   {below in Albanian}
       < .. in his long-lived son
       who lives today in this life\
       is hidden his father
       these are the words of truth\>
    thus is this~

25. FT: there must be yes\   {soft voice}

26. Baba: **thus** from that poin- it does\

27. FT: \but from a spiritual [point of view

28. Baba: [spiritual point of view\~

29. FT: . hmm .. but **these days it is harder**~
because as for this
God willing it will not be lost [however

30. Baba: [much-

31. FT: **it is not clear**\

32. Baba: LOOK HERE~
       ah- how materialism progresses\

33. FT: . hmmmm

34. Baba: . as much as materialism progresses~
    . the spiritual declines\
    bu- it is hidden it declines but~
    ah it declines\
    it is not seen but~
    it is not lost

35. FT: ummm
36. Baba: gene var\
                ama kim bilir ne vakıt gelir zamani ki
                - aç- açabilir gene\
                . anladın mi?
37. FT: .. ama Bektasşism Baba~
                sakladi- buuu-
                .. bu babalar sakladı\
                bu murşitler sakladı\
                ki— .. [bizim
38. Baba: [bu-
39. FT: ·   mirathımız da~
                şey protection verdiler
40. Baba: ya
41. FT: ki~
                ellerden\
                ellere~
                ellerden\
42. Baba: ellere~
                gayip olmadi\
43. FT: olmadı\
44. Baba: şimdiye kadar\
45. FT: şimdiye kadar\
46. Baba: yaa\
47. FT: ama bugünler Baba?
48. Baba: bugunler~
                . bakalım\   {all in softer voice}
                ne olur\
                        < .... la yalim ul-gayipe illa-allah> {in Arabic}
                yani~ gayip olani~
                . Allahtan başka bilmezdır birisi\
49. FT: {warm chuckle}
                oldu [Baba
50. Baba: [{joins in chuckle}
51. FT: işte bizim ellerimizde değil\
52. Baba: evet\

35. FT: ummm
36. Baba: it is still there\
            but who knows when the time will come
            -for it to grow again\
            . have you understood?
37. FT: .. but Bektashism Baba~
            it preserved it-
            .. these babas preserved it\
            these murshids preserved it\
            so that— .. [our
38. Baba: [this-
39. FT: heritage as well~
            that they gave "protection"
40. Baba: ya
41. FT: so that~
            from hands\
            to hands~
            from hands\
42. Baba: to hands~
            it was not lost\
43. FT: not lost\
44. Baba: up to now\
45. FT: up to now\
46. Baba: yaa\
47. FT: but in these days Baba?
48. Baba: in these days~
            let us see\   {all in softer voice}
            what will be\
                < .... la yalim ul-gayipe illa-allah> {in Arabic}
            that is~ . of what has disappeared~
            . no one but God knows\
49. FT: {warm chuckle}
            so it is [Baba
50. Baba: [{joins in chuckle}
51. FT: **thus** it is not in our hands\
52. Baba: no\

What then is the interactive structure of this episode? A cursory description of the interaction could be that it is made up of a series of four question-and-answer passages in which I ask and Baba answers (first figure).

Second Episode as a Series of Question-Answer Passages

turns 1–6

(I see there are no murshids in America)

(. . . people of the way have been destroyed everywhere)

turns 7–28

(will it change, what do you think)

(. . . nothing is ever lost . . . inside the son the father is hidden, the Albanian couplet, pantheism)

turns 29–36

(but these days it is harder . . . God Willing it will not be lost, however, it is not clear)

(LOOK here how materialism progresses . . . the spiritual declines but it is not lost)

turns 37–52

(but Bektashism preserved it . . . but in these days Baba, these days Baba)

(. . . let us see, Arabic "of what has disappeared no one but God knows")

Yet closer reading shows that only the second of my above comments is a question. The others are better described as references (Goffman, 1981) or comments (Ochs, 1983) to which a response is expected. And as the character of the response is open to Baba, "answer" would be too specific a term. But even to describe these more accurately as a series of "reference-response passages" still misses the dynamic of the episode.

The interaction of the episode is better summarized by the moves in the next figure.

Interactional Moves of Second Episode

turns 1–6

my initiating reference

Baba's response

turns 7–28

my transitional reference

Baba's response, Baba's initiation of closure

turns 29–36

| my withholding of affirmation of closure | Baba's reframing Baba's direct request for affirmation of closure |

turns 37–52

| my second withholding of affirmation and drawn-out reframing my affirmations of closure | Baba's joining in new frame Baba's third initiation of closure Baba's confirmation of my affirmations |

Thus the first two passages (turns 1–6, 7–28) reflect the conventional order of interaction between Baba and myself, while the last two passages (turns 29–36, 37–52) include reframings by both Baba and myself before yielding to closure. To build context for my withholding of affirmation in turns 29 and 31, I will first describe the more conventional preceding passages. As mentioned, my initiating reference was drawn from a response of Baba's in the preceding episode.

1. FT: .... so Baba~
           .. that~ . I see that they are lacking\
                                   \in America\
           . that there are no murshids\

Baba responded with:

2. Baba: there are none here\
           such ones\ spirit- not in America~
           in all places now there are no longer\
3. FT: hmmm
4. Baba: that is~ those~
           who hold to spiritual ways~
5. FT: yes\
6. Baba: only~
           ah- they are spiritual persons~
           . or <people of the WAY>\
           people of the way~ they are neither here
           not anywhere now des-
           in America it is destroyed~
           whatever yes~

> in Turkey too they have been destroyed~
> and in Albania destroyed~
> in every place it is this way\

In this response, Baba expands on my reference in two ways. First, he expands on my geographic reference of there being no murshids in America to this being the case "everywhere." Second, he rephrases my point, except that whereas I said there were no "murshids," Baba uses three other terms:

"manevi yolunu tutanlar"
(those who hold to spiritual ways)

"ruhani adamlar"
(spiritual persons)

"ehl-i tarik"
(people of the way)

There is a progression in these terms from the first, which has a Turkish verbal base (*tutanlar*), to the third, which, is a Persian genitive construction. In the Turkish context, the progression moves toward a more syntactically marked phrase. Further, of the three main Islamic language groups of the Near East—the Arabs, the Persians, and the Turks—it is the Persians who are most associated with Sufism and from whom many of its terms come. Thus this progression also moves toward a more particularly Sufi terminology.

These rephrasings can also be understood as substitutions for my term "murshid." Substitution is a most important phenomenon in language learning: it sets up a contextual frame for contrast, as here, but it is also part of the process of creating sets of semantic domains. Elinor Ochs (1983) claims that for children the creation of lexical sets through substitution is instrumental in developing discourse that is not bound by the here and now. Instead of being tied to the immediate context of what the child sees and hears, with the advent of substitution, the child can draw on background knowledge as well.

Baba, in his response, moves into more Sufi terms. For me this expansion of the semantic domain, parallels and points to what is hoped to be an expansion of experience toward the Sufi world.

Baba's response ends with another progression in which he reiterates his point that there are no "people of the way" anywhere today. He expands upon "not anywhere" as "not in America," but also not in Turkey nor in Albania. Baba and I hail respectively from Albania and America, but why mention Turkey? The answer is, I believe, related to Baba's additional comment that not only do these "people of the way" not exist, but they have been destroyed.

In 1826 the Ottoman Sultan Mahmud II ordered the destruction of the Bektashi Order. At that time, tekkes were burned and babas killed or exiled. Some fled to Albania. Then the Order built up again in Turkey, only to be made illegal once more in Turkey, this time by Atatürk in 1925. The headquarters was subsequently moved to Albania. But after World War II, the Communists took over in Albania and the Bektashis were again killed or suppressed.

Thus Baba's description of the destruction of "people of the way" from Turkey to Albania reflects twice the historical direction of destruction of the Order. His geographic elaboration is therefore a particularly Bektashi understanding of "everywhere."

It is interesting that this elaboration came after his series of terms leading into "ehl-i tarik" (people of the way). It is as if the first progression to more Sufi terminology triggered the second progression to a more Bektashi understanding of "everywhere."

After Baba's above response, the second passage (turns 7 to 28) transpired, beginning with my question:

7. FT: ..... will it change- will it change Baba
          what do you think?

Early in Baba's response to this he put forward an adage that was expressly framed as coming from Bektashism:

8. Baba: ahhh it
          it is not clear\
          . but there is something\
                              \in Bektashism~
          everything is hid- < nothing is ever lost>\

Baba then searched for specific others who voiced forms of this adage. The ones he brought up: a philosopher (whose name he remembered two lessons later), Naim Frashëri (a nineteenth-century Albanian poet), and Ni-yazi Mısri (a sixteenth-century Sufi poet) show a certain progression, from philosopher to poet. This also parallels the progression from outer to in-ward, from knowledge of the mind to knowledge of the heart.

Baba's initial framing of the adage and his subsequent attributions and quotations potentially set off his involvement in the discussion. In terms of Goffman's "production format" (Goffman, 1981), in which the notion of speaker is spun out into one or combinations of three statuses (of "animator," as merely a reciter of someone else's words; of "principal," as one who is committed to what the words say; or of "author," as one who has chosen both the sentiments and the words), Baba thus set up the possibility that in the discussion he was perhaps only an animator, or that at least his personal involvement was somehow restricted.

This framing and quoting, however, which in our rhetorical tradition can appear either as a restriction on commitment on the part of the speaker, or as a display of erudition, can have other significance in other rhetorical traditions. For, as Baba later told me, "How can we know of the spiritual world except by those who have seen it?" Such quotations, in-stead of merely lending support to a proposition, can be a form of proof. Furthermore, Baba later interpreted another instance of his quoting from others not to imply that he reserved his own opinion, but rather that it was not only he who held the expressed opinion.

Baba then elucidated the pantheism of the Albanian couplet, leading into an "işte" phrase. As mentioned earlier, "işte" phrases in Baba's lessons with me, especially when they follow quotations and explanations, fre-quently signal closure of the episode. In most episodes, here I would have shown acceptance of closure and the episode would have ended.

However, this is where this episode stands out. After Baba's "işte" phrase, instead of going along with closure, I made another response-eliciting reference:

29. FT: . hmm .. but in **these days** it is harder~
           because as for this
           God willing it will not be lost [however
30. Baba: [much-
31. FT: it is not clear\

Baba responded to this with a swift frame change away from talk of phi-losophers and pantheism to talk of materialism.

32. Baba: LOOK HERE~
        ah- how materialism progresses\
33. FT: . hmmmm
34. Baba: . as much as materialism progresses~
        the spiritual declines\
        bu- it is hidden it declines but~
        ah it declines\
        it is not seen but~
        it is not lost\
35. FT: ummm
36. Baba: it is still there\
        but who knows when the time will come
        -for it to grow again\
        . have you understood?

This reframing on Baba's part represents a departure from elaborating within the Bektashi tradition. But it still maintains the same point of the earlier response, namely, that spiritual life will not be lost. In this later response, however, a cause or at the very least a co-existing phenomenon with the decline of the spiritual is presented in materialism. And, more in line with persuasive talk in my rhetorical background, Baba insists directly that the decline of the spiritual is not final.

Notice also the unusual emphasis with which Baba began this reframing, "LOOK HERE," and the explicit close to his talk on materialism, "Have you understood?" But instead of acknowledging whether I had understood, again I questioned. This insistence in questioning was unusual in the lessons. Baba's strong responses to my remarks highlight not only my insistence but also the expected structure of the episode. The brackets of the lesson are negotiated ones, and when Baba initiates closure he expects acknowledgment of this.

This particular sort of acknowledgment I have referred to as an "affirmation." Affirmations have much in common with the "hmmm"s or "yes"s[5] that are found throughout the lesson and many interactions. These serve as evidence that the addressee is listening and is following, and may encourage the speaker to continue. But an affirmation as I define it here also has the special property of signaling acceptance of initiation of closure of the episode. Thus the structure of the episode is one of reference and response, whose final sets include initiation of closure plus affirmation.

Structure of an Episode

my initiating reference
$\longrightarrow$ Baba's response

Baba's initiation of closure
$\longrightarrow$ my affirmation

In the second episode, however, I withhold affirmation not once but twice. The second time is after Baba explicitly asked if I had understood. Instead of responding to this directly, I, too, reframed:

37. FT: .. but Bektashism Baba~
            it preserved it-
            .. these babas preserved it\
            these murshids preserved it\
            so that- .. [our
38. Baba: [this-
39. FT: heritage as well~
            that they gave "protection"
40. Baba: ya
41. FT: so that~
            from hands\
            to hands~
            from hands\
42. Baba: to hands~
            it was not lost\
43. FT: not lost\
44. Baba: up to now\
45. FT: up to now\
46. Baba: yaa\
47. FT: but in these days Baba?

I not only reframed my question relating to the survival of spiritual understanding in our times, I also drew it out over seventeen lines.

Such spreading out of a proposition over a sequence of utterances has been described as a defining feature of distressed communication in general and of caretaker speech in particular, the problem of the caretaker being to secure the child's attention.[6] I see here the initial spreading out of the proposition to draw attention, but soon Baba picks up on my concern, which he signals by building on my series of "hand to hand" and adding the crucial "it was not lost." As we both continue, echoing and latching onto each other's utterances, the effect is quite the opposite of distress. The actual effect is to mirror our alignment over an unspoken but utterly significant matter. This matter is the continuity of the tekke and how to face not knowing how it will continue after Baba's death. There is not yet a successor to take over when Baba dies. Four or five people of different degrees of religious maturity and community perspicacity have appeared over the years, but they have either died or proven themselves not suited.

With an understanding of the seriousness of the topic we have broached, the episode takes on different hues. I see the earlier response-eliciting references as being general ones. At some point, the more personal concern must have come up and I needed to pull Baba to a more personal frame. I signaled this by not acknowledging Baba's "işte" phrase and by voicing a third reference. Baba assumed it was the form of his response that I could not follow and therefore reframed in a more modern way. But it was not a different rhetorical form that I sought; rather it was the personal focus. When I was able to put this in the context of Bektashism and the personal (note my use of pronoun "our" of "our heritage" in turns 37 and 39), Baba quickly saw my concern. He responded by playing into my syntax, words, and rhythmic patterns so closely that although we are two people, the result is one move.

After our dance of phrases, Baba's response, all in a softer voice, is humble and personal to the ground of his being.

48. Baba: in these days~
                                        {all in softer voice}

          let us see\
          what will be\
                    < .... la yalim ul-gayipe illa-allah> {in Arabic}
          that is~ . of what has disappeared~
          . no one but God knows\

The Arabic of this response refers of course to the Qur'an. In addition, the message refers to the submission of human beings to God, which is the essential understanding of "Islam" and what it means to be a "Muslim," that is, "submitted to God."

In terms of the episode, this response shares characteristics of earlier

responses. Like Baba's first response, in which he expanded on my reference of there being no murshids in America, here Baba builds on my
words "but in these days?" Like the second response, in which Baba
quoted the adage and Naim's words, here Baba also recites a distant text
(the Qur'an). What distinguishes the response here, though, is Baba's involvement, seen in the integration of our expression of the question, in his
movement into a softer, more collusive voice, and also in his use of the
pronoun—"let us see." With its quotation in Arabic and brief elucidation,
I also see this response as yet a third initiation of closure.

In earlier discussion of internal brackets of episodes, I mentioned that
quotations of distant texts by Baba are often found around closure.
Among quotations, those from the Qur'an are particularly powerful. Not
only is the Arabic distinctive in a sea of Turkish, but the Qur'an is the
ground of all legitimacy in Islam. After Baba recites from the Qur'an, not
much can be added. This then is a particularly effective initiation of
closure.

Missing from this initiation of closure is Baba's use of an "işte"
phrase. That an "işte" is implied, however, can be inferred from my affirmations that immediately follow Baba's elucidation of the Arabic line:

49. FT: {warm chuckle}
      so it is [Baba
50. Baba: [{joins in chuckle}
51. FT: **thus** it is not in our hands\
52. Baba: no\

Certainly my comment (turn 49) "so it is Baba" is broadly affirming. As if
to mirror my understanding that Baba has initiated closure, in my next
line I affirm closure with an "işte" myself: "thus it is not in our hands"
(turn 51). This last utterance refers to both my questions on the future of
"people of the way" as well as the more personal situation after Baba's
death.

Yet what does the chuckling signify in this context? I think my chuckling was a sign of relief that Baba had understood my concern of what was
to happen after his death. This is a concern that is difficult to talk about
directly, and yet Baba showed me that he understood it by joining in
my last question. And further, with the Arabic line, he shared with me
how he faces this. But I also see my chuckling as a sign of pleasure in our

play and verbal coming together. Baba's joining in the chuckling further showed our shared pleasure. My following comment, "thus it is not in our hands"—

> işte **bizim** elle**rimiz**de değil\
> (thus **our** hands—**our**—in is not)

—then recaptured Baba's point, while its optionally multiple references to "our" in the Turkish emphasize the shared nature of our concern.

Overall, the process of reframings on both our parts as we negotiated a more personal focus on our earlier topic showed our responsiveness to each other. This responsiveness is both a sign and a feature of our attunement. By way of contrast, recall the approach of the professor in his interview with Baba the same week as the Hizir lesson. He initiated talk head-on by asking about the survival of the tekke, and although he brought up the topic several times during the interview, it was with the grace and flexibility of a bulldozer.[7] But then he did not have twelve years of previous dialogues to build on.

Finally, though, notice Baba's last utterance of the episode. It is a "no" of agreement which serves as an affirmation of my affirmation. Such a move I term a "confirmation." It is as if my affirmations are also references that require from Baba a response.

Openings and Closings of Early Episodes

> in which the description of episode structure is refined with examples of uncomfortably vulnerable openings and strangely aphoristic closings

In the previous section I looked closely at one of the early episodes in the Hizir lesson. There I described how Baba responded to my initiating references, either with progressions that led to Sufi terms or with juxtapositions of distant texts in the form of adages or sayings that he then anchored by attribution and explanation. Through interaction described as a "withholding of affirmation," I developed an expected structure of interaction of the episode that can be summarized in the figure.

Structure of an Episode

Opening sequence
    my reference
        $\longrightarrow$ Baba's response
               $\longrightarrow$ my reference
               (transition)

Body
    Baba's responses

Closing sequence
    Baba's initiation of closure
    (commonly with discourse marker "işte")
               $\longrightarrow$ my affirmation
                  $\longrightarrow$ Baba's confirmation

In this manner of defining the episode the boundaries are stated in more abstract terms. But is this so much *safsata* (sophistry) as Baba would put it? Does this model fit other episodes and does it lead to greater understanding of our interaction?

VULNERABILITIES OF OPENINGS

Openings of episodes, which are generally characterized by hedging, pausing, faltering syntax, and often protracted development of reference, are among my most vulnerable and unsure times. Of the seven episodes in the first hour of the lesson, there were three whose openings were particularly uncomfortable. I examine these, not from orneriness, but from the understanding that situations of interactional difficulty can be most revealing of relations between people.

As might be expected, the initial episode is among the most uncomfortable. Certainly if openings of episodes are times when I am most aware of my ignorance and of the imposition that questioning implies, then the opening of the entire lesson is even more so. And later in the lesson, openings do not necessarily become smoother. For example, the opening of the fifth episode brought another sort of difficulty, while the opening of the fourth episode was so problematic that Baba and I spent most of the episode in remedy and mediation of my unfortunate outset.

In the initial episode, I broached the topic of the relationship of murshid and talib in a general way. Baba responded with the saying in Arabic that "the murshid is to the talib as the Prophet to the community." But then I was unable to provide a transitional reference that Baba would build on. Talk subsided.

So I tried again to introduce discussion of the relationship of murshid and talib, this time reframed in terms of my society. Baba immediately modified my statement, in which I had spoken of the murshid-talib relationship, to speak only in terms of the murshid. Then again things petered out as Baba closed discussion.

Yet a third time I brought up the murshid and talib, this time in the frame of Christianity. Here Baba joined in my transition and finally the discussion was launched.

During the earlier uncomfortable times of reframing, Baba had not been overly solicitous, but neither had he been discouraging. Through this I had gained practice in reframing—a skill in which Baba excells. This reframing is a sort of attunement on my part, as I knew that Baba would not discourse until he achieved what was to him the right entree.

In the following episode, that is, the second episode which was discussed in the last section, I mediated the awkwardness of the opening by drawing my initiating reference from a response of Baba's in the previous episode. Baba expanded on my reference. Building on this, I was able to make a transition that Baba carried into discussion.

The fifth episode was similar to the second in that I began with a reference that Baba immediately expanded. There I started:

FT: ..... hey so BaBA~
        it means that
        .. in Bektashi history~
Baba: . hhm
FT: ... it is full of murshids

Baba responded by stretching my reference beyond Bektashism and reminding me of the murshids in other religions including those of ancient India, of the Kabala in Judaism, and of ancient Greece. The difference between this expansion and Baba's earlier expansion in the second episode was length. In the second episode, Baba had expanded on my opening for fifteen seconds. In the fifth episode, he went on for four minutes. By the time we finished with the expansion, I had forgotten what I had been leading up to.

The opening of the fourth episode, however, was the most problematic. Here it was not an issue of reframing to Baba's satisfaction, or even of keeping a train of thought. The problem here was that I began by requesting what I had no right to request. This request (in bold) was housed in a typical opening sequence:

1. FT: .. do you know~
          .. hey let's have a look\
{checks tape}
          as for me **what I like are stories**\
                                      \one thing
          I like are stories\
2. Baba: yaa
3. FT: for example that one on Musa and Hizir~
          com-
4. Baba: yes
5. FT: -pletely (tells) of the mur-
6. Baba: -shid
7. FT: what he is\
          are there others Baba~

To this innocently straightforward question, Baba responded:

8. Baba: ohh- you know if you
          speak well on this story~
          it will finish half your thesis\

With this response Baba side-stepped my immediate question about other stories, for, as I now understand, stories cannot be ordered up like scrambled eggs in a restaurant. Baba only tells stories in the process of making a point. In this sense they are more like parables.[8]

To request a parable does damage to the parable's way of meaning, for the meaning of a parable is in its recasting of the situation of its addressee. So too with Baba's stories. They cannot be called up by direct request of listeners. Rather it is Baba's perception of the resonance of a listener's situation with a story that leads him to recount it, and of course reshape it. For example, in earlier lessons, Baba had told me the story of

Hizir and Musa in the context of my own impatience. Then in this lesson he told the story of Hizir and Musa to show how the murshid is an intermediary. And later, at the end of this episode, Baba told the story of the ant going on pilgrimage[9]—in the context of explaining the "perfection" of a murshid.

All of which is to say I had made an error in asking for stories. Baba of course did not tell me this outright. Instead, by not answering my question in the way I had expected, Baba initiated a gradual process of self-correction. This behavior is consistent with formulations of "repair," or correction of misunderstanding or error, in studies of conversation in which "other-initiations overwhelmingly yield self-corrections."[10] But research into repair in conversation has understandably focused on repair that takes place within at most two conversational turns of what was repaired. This research concludes that the tendency is for self-correction over other-correction (imagine the tyranny or dissolution of relationships that would result were other-correction the rule), and also that this self-correction most often occurs within the same turn as that which it corrects.

In contrast, although Baba initiated repair in the turn following my unfortunate opening in episode 4, it was not until four turns later that I followed up with a sort of self-correction. And while understanding is a matter separable from self-correction, for one can attempt correction knowing only that something was not right, it is interesting to note that I did not understand what was wrong with requesting stories until whole lessons later.

This study differs from conversational studies of repair in that it has a long-term view of interaction of the participants. It also differs in that, unlike most sociologically based studies, the ongoing relationship of the participants is of focal interest. Finally, it differs in that Baba, unlike the man-on-the-street voices of most sociological studies, is an artist of repair. For example, a misattribution I made in the first minute of the lesson was subtly corrected by Baba forty turns later. It is as if Baba has been trained in strategies of subtle repair. Theologically the task of the murshid could be construed as one of repair—repair of blindness to the coherence of life.

Baba's deflective response in this episode signaled to me that I had not chosen the right way to proceed. Here was that minimal conversational attunement in which one is sensitive to the need to reframe one's remarks without necessarily understanding why this should be done.

My response was therefore a general remedy in which I acknowledged my need for Baba's help. Mirroring this dependence on Baba, I went into Baba's dialect in this remedy by using a locative postposition (*tape'de koy-mak*) the way he does, instead of the more standard Turkish dative post-position (*tape'e koymak*) I would ordinarily use.

11. FT: .. so Baba\
            I . whatever .
            I put it on tape this\
            . I will go home\
12. Baba: ya
13. FT: I will write\
            again I will bring it back~
            we will speak about it is that possible?
14. Baba: -possible
            sure\
15. FT: because I want to really find the meaning\

Baba's response, which was not said with irony, was a mediation of my remedy:

16. Baba: everything is possible
          for Frances~

   Baba's use of my name is extremely rare and therefore most effective in drawing my attention and signaling closeness. This called for a me-diation, here a humbling response on my part, as did Baba's speaking of the future. In Islamic societies, talk of the future is frequently mediated by the phrase "inşallah" ("if God pleases," that is, "God willing").

17. FT: God willing
18. Baba: everything is possible
19. FT: -God willing Baba\

But after a few "ya"s Baba followed with:

22. Baba: I want that
          it be high high you- that you be so\

23. FT: {appreciative laugh}
           ahhhh Baba\
24. Baba: {also laughing along}

Baba's wish for me that I rise high again called forth a mediation from me in which I acknowledged my debt to Baba for all my understanding. I did this in the form of a long narrative on how I first came to the tekke[11] and how I became the student of Baba.[12]

   In summary, the pattern of redress in the exchanges in the episode so far has been as in the figure.

Summary of Redress Thus Far

1. my error
   (ask for other stories)
                                    Baba's deflective response

2. my attempt at remedy through
   acknowledgment of my need of Baba
                                    Baba's mediation of that remedy
                                    (all is possible for Frances)

3. my mediation of Baba's mediation
   (inşallah—God willing)
                                    Baba's continuing hope for me
                                    (to rise high)

4. acknowledgment of that hope
   (appreciative laughter)
                                    Baba's laughter

5. my mediation of that hope
   (through the telling of narrative)

   The dynamic of this interchange is that as Baba helped me right myself in my own face (for I know I have erred), he demonstrated his support to such a degree that I felt impelled to mediate or compensate for a new imbalance created by that help.

   With my narrative, Baba early recognized it for the mediation it was and said simply, "thank you." Once the narrative was begun though, I kept going until I got to the point when Baba Bayram, a baba who was a close friend of Baba and who also lived at the tekke, suggested that I study with Baba. This is a key passage because the point of my story was how fortunate I was to study with Baba. To initiate closure in the story I repeated the point two times.

47. FT: Baba Bayram said
                why don't you come
                and take lessons with Baba
      do you remember this?
48. Baba: ya
49. FT: Baba Bayram said that
                you should take lessons
                with Baba Rejeb

The tables were turned with my telling the story instead of Baba. Here it was I who asked for affirmation. Baba responded:

50. Baba: that means∼
      so it's to be understood that it was Baba Bayram
      who assigned to me this "misfortune"
51. FT and Baba: {shared laughter}

This was a remarkable affirmation because it both referred to the point of my narrative and offered a mediation of that point. As such, it facilitated Baba's and my coming together in laughter.

Earlier I mentioned that shared laughter was common in closing sections of episodes. This laughter effectively closes my narrative. Following Baba's affirmation were more mediations of mediations until as I was saying how I hoped my writing on the Bektashis would be positive for the tekke, for my society, and that even those at the university might learn something, Baba interjected that perhaps they would be interested. I added "so much," to which Baba slyly inserted "sophistry." My point is that Baba again used humor to break the chain of mediations. I followed with a joke of my own, after which there was more shared laughter. With its association with closings, and its releasing and binding nature, this laughter certainly seemed like a winding down of a most unusual episode.

In what I see as an affirmation of this movement toward closure, my next comment was the aphoristic phrase

the teacher who truly teaches
must be a murshid

This is hardly an earthshattering observation, but it surely served to second Baba's attempt to stop the mediations we had gotten into. The distinctive form and tone of the aphorism replicated nothing that had come before in this episode. This aphoristic form, which is for me a distinctly Bektashi one, is a sort of attunement to Baba's adages and quotations that he often cites in closing an episode. The assurance such a form implies also showed that I had finally accepted as sufficient the mediation of my opening error.

"Reach" in Closings

In the previous section I described episode openings that were "at risk" or vulnerable in various ways. I ended that discussion by contrasting the aphoristic affirmation in the closing section of the fourth episode with the preceding remedies, mediations, and opening of that episode.

The contrast between my opening and my affirmation in that episode, in terms of form and assurance, turns out to be a common contrast across the first seven episodes of the lesson. Openings are places of uncertainty, places of possible affront, places where misunderstandings can easily occur. The hedging and pausing in openings reflect this. Affirmations, however, coming as they do after Baba's initiations of closure, are places of integration where I acknowledge closure in compact and fluent forms: single words, laughter, simple phrases, or integrated clauses including aphorism.

In particular, the affirmations that are of the distinctive aphoristic form—the terse, syntactically marked, assuratively stated affirmations—are maximally different from the openings of episodes. They are also a puzzle. Why should I shift into this aphoristic form, this "second cousin to a cliché," which I would avoid in English? To investigate this I look at these affirmations in the context of their episode, with special emphasis on Baba's following confirmations.

In confirmations, Baba acknowledges my affirmations and sometimes modifies and extends them. Such modifications and extensions provide perspective on the affirmations. Together, the affirmation and confirmation pairs serve as special loci of attunement.

The distinctive character of the affirmation-confirmation sequence in general relates to the "reach" of the preceding utterance. As defined, the preceding utterance of an affirmation is Baba's initiation of closure of the episode. These initiations of closure often have the reach of the whole episode, or in the case of adages and quotations from the Qur'an, they have the reach of an eternal truth. Such reach is contagious, or at least stretching for following utterances.

"Reach" is a critical concept in accounting for the flexibility of talk. It embodies the understanding that a speaker in a situation can respond to all manner of features of that situation. For example, when two people meet and greet: "How are you?" "Hi," the "Hi" is not a nonsequitur. Rather the reach of the "Hi" is a response to the presence of the other, not to his or her words per se (Goffman, 1981). Or, within the bounds of talk, a speaker can choose to respond to an entire set of exchanges rather than just the immediately preceding one.

In his essay on the organization of talk, Goffman (1981) states:

> Standard sequences are involved, but these are not sequences of statement and reply, but rather sequences at a higher level, ones regarding choice with respect to reach and to the construing of what is reached for.[13]

A familiar example of such a "sequence at a higher level" is the stretch and variability of reach in the closing section of the second episode. There Baba initiated closure with the Qur'anic "of the hidden no one but God knows." The reach of this is to the entire episode framed in an eternal truth. My following affirmation in that episode had three parts. First I chuckled. Clearly this response did not parallel the reach of the Qur'anic line; I read it rather as an expression of relief and pleasure that Baba had understood what I was asking about. Then I said, "so it is Baba," in which my reach is to Baba's implied way of facing the unknown and to the closing of the episode. Finally, I added, "thus it is not in our hands" as a more personal statement, but with reach similar to that of the Qur'anic line.

Baba's confirmation of this was a simple "yes." In the three closings of episodes that I affirm in aphoristic fashion (episode 1, episode 4, and episode 6), Baba's confirmations are more extensive.

The first episode is the longest one (sixteen minutes) of the whole lesson, as well as being rich in narrative and adage. Baba initiated closure in this episode with the adage on the talib being like a corpse in the hands of the murshid. He then asked if I understood and noted that there were many people who had no knowledge of such things. I responded with the affirmation that what Baba had just told me was quite different (from the Sunni way without an intermediary), and that, as was clear in Baba's talk,

150. FT: <to each talib there should be a murshid>\
151. Baba: is a murshid\
152. FT: that is
                      <without a murshid one sees nothing>\

The reach of my affirmation here is similar to Baba's preceding point that there are many people who do not know of these things. Notice, too, how I restate the aphorism from a positive phrasing—"to each talib there should be a murshid"—to a negative phrasing—"without a murshid one sees nothing." Baba responded:

153. Baba: without a murshid~
           .. ah- we say~
                < he who goes on the way without a murshid~
                ah—is like a ship without a captain>
           . it is like that\
154. FT: heyy that's true\   {with chuckle}
155. Baba: himself~
           .. a ship or a car without a man cannot go-
           can it go
           no\
156. FT: no\
157. Baba: therefore~
           ahh-
                < on the spiritual way~
                without a murshid
                a person does not progress>\

Baba's response to my aphorism was prefaced by "we say." He then proceeded to give: a restatement ("he who goes on the way without a murshid is like a ship without a captain"), an explanation (which brought in the parallel with a car and driver), and then a second restatement ("without a murshid a person does not progress on the spiritual way").
    The first restatement builds directly on my aphorism by using the

previous phrase, "without a murshid," as the first phrase of the restatement. The explanation also builds on my "motor city" society and its cars (recall the tekke lies outside Detroit), while the second restatement significantly adds *ruhani yolunda* or "on the spiritual way." This mention of "the way" was missing from my formulation. It is important because the point of the murshid is to lead a talib on this way.

Baba also reinforced the negative phrasing that I had moved into myself (turn 152) in that his restatements and explanation refer to what does not happen if one has no murshid. Thus Baba's response to my aphorisic affirmation works to bring my words more in line with Bektashi expression.

A second instance of an aphoristic affirmation was in the fourth episode. This was the episode that began with my misguided request for more stories. Most of the episode (five minutes of a seven-minute total episode time) was then taken up with remedy and mediation and mediation of mediation. Baba twice made jokes which temporarily stopped the back-and-forth of mediation. To the second of these, I responded with a joke that served as an outset of the affirmation. I then followed with an aphorisim:

FT: .. as I see it Baba~
        <it must be that the teacher
        who truly teaches is a murshid>
Baba: ya that's true\
        certainly a murshid\
        a murshid- of course a murshid
        but in saying a murshid~
        I mean a "perfected murshid" {murşid-i kamil}
        such that
                <to each murshid do not give your heart
                he teaches only false ways
FT: yes
Baba: as for the perfected murshid
        his way is most truly smooth>

There is special attunement in Baba's response to my affirmation. First Baba made sure that by "murshid" I had in mind a true murshid—in the Persian phrase that Baba then used—a *murşid-i kamil*, or a "perfected murshid." He captured this caveat by reciting a modified couplet from a nefes by Niyazi Mısri (sixteenth century):

Her murşide dil verme gıl
yalnız safta öğretir

Murşid-i kâmil olanın
gayet yolu asan imiş

* * * * *

To each murshid do not give your heart
He teaches only false ways

As for the perfected murshid
His way is most truly smooth

When Baba recited the lines from the nefes, though, he modified them. In particular, the usual version of the second line is *yolunu sarpa uğradır* ("his way will lead to difficulty [steepness]"), which is more coherent with the final line. What Baba's modification (*yalnız safta öğretir,* or "he teaches only false ways") did, however, was resonate with our immediately preceding interaction. He picked up the word he had just used in his humorous initiation of closing, *safsata* (shortened to *safta*) or "sophistry," and coupled it with the verb I had just used in my affirmation—*öğretmek,* "to teach."

This modifying of the nefes drew my attention so much that I did not realize Baba was reciting from a nefes. My "yes" between the lines of the nefes, as well as my initial transcription of this section, showed that I had not perceived the lines as from another text. Perhaps sensing my distraction, Baba then amplified the phrase "perfected murshid" from the last line of the nefes with a short narrative:

Baba: oh don't think that we are perfect
\we are not so perfect~
however nevertheless~
we work at becoming perfect\
FT: yes
Baba: how is it the ant~
tries~
to whatever- that it go on the pilgrimage\
and so\
as much strength as it has~

this much it expends of that strength\
that God {Sufi term} give it more strength~
and it will go that much forward\
that's how it is\

Thus to my aphoristic affirmation, Baba presented a confirmation in the form of a modified nefes. He further commented on the nefes with an abbreviated narrative.

The last episode with an aphoristic affirmation is episode 6. Briefly, in this episode I opened with a sequence that led to asking why it is that we know of great murshids from their talibs. Baba answered, "because of inspiration" (*üfürüş*). As a way of explaining "inspiration," Baba then immediately told a short narrative, again from a negative perspective, about a baba who did not write poetry.

Baba: . they said to one\
                    \to a baba or whatever\
        .. how is it he said
        ... you . you haven't written anything
        not a nefes-
        or anything\
                    . oh they haven't given me anything
                    that I write he said
        what do you mean given\
                    . because WHATEVER comes
                                    \that a
                    perfect one says~
                    . THAT is received\
                                    \received that is
                    in-come\

In his explanation of this story, Baba allowed as how this "in-come" is from God or one's teacher—in other words, "through an intermediary." This connects directly to the whole Hizir and Musa story from the first episode, whose point was that the murshid was an intermediary.

After this explanation, Baba initiated closure with an "işte" phrase. I responded with an aphoristic affirmation that Baba immediately modified:

Baba: thus it is they\
FT: that means that
                        < great poets~
Baba: .. but-
FT: are disciples>\ {muritler, like talib}
Baba: ah ah-
       that is great po-
       SPIRITUAL poets
FT: of course
Baba: [that means-
FT: [I mean to say that Baba
Baba: ya
FT: <great~ spiritual po-
Baba: poets~
FT: -s~
       are disciples>\
Baba: yes\
       **.... certainly there are those who have said
       this**
                                    {in lower pitch, even pace}
                    <what appears to our eyes~
                        that we write\
                    what is given~
                        that we say\
                    what we feel in our hearts~
                        that we disclose\>

Again, an aphoristically stated affirmation had led to a confirmation in the form of a nefes. The nefes that Baba was referring to here is one by Mehmet Ali Hilmi Dede Baba (nineteeth century), the complete text of which is in Appendix B.

Baba's prefacing comment to his nefes, however, was not what I had expected. It had been with pride in my understanding that I had asserted that "the great spiritual poets are disciples." But instead of patting me on the back for my growing understanding, Baba had responded that "certainly there are those who have said this." It took the wind out of my sails.

Yet in a later lesson, when I had asked Baba about the purpose of quoting others' words, Baba had said that it was to show that not only he thought this way, but others did as well. In responding to my aphorism with the comment that others had said as much, Baba was confirming that my affirmation fit with Bektashi tradition. It was as if he were stepping aside to link my words with this tradition.

Thus Baba's words, "certainly there are those who have said this," are only disparaging to those who, like myself, link art and intelligence with originality. We share, to use Harold Bloom's phrase, an "anxiety of influence." However, in Baba's way, as made clear by his understanding of inspiration as "in-come" from his murshid, there is rather an anxiety of noninfluence. It is in this tradition that the great Sufi poet Rumi (thirteenth century) wrote a collection of poetry and entitled it the "Collected Works of Shemseddin Tabrizi," Tabrizi being Rumi's teacher.

Returning to the question of the occurrence of the aphoristic form in affirmations of closings, it is noteworthy that in the three cases described above, Baba confirmed by moving toward and then into actual nefes. (Apart from these confirmations, Baba moved into a nefes only one other place in the lesson.) It is as if these terse, syntactically marked, and assuratively phrased clauses suggest to Baba a reach to Bektashi forms. He responds with similar reach, and because he is a Bektashi baba and reciter of hundreds of nefes, he can call up appropriate nefes that move my aphorisms closer to this specialized form of interaction.

But why did I voice these affirmations in aphoristic form in the first place? Here I look not at the following confirmations but at the preceding bodies of the episodes. In other words, what do episodes 1, 4, and 6 have in common that might trigger formally similar affirmations?

I suggest that episodes 1 and 6 have in common a specifically Bektashi resonance of inter-lesson and intra-lesson attunement. In episode 1 there is Bektashi attunement across the two adages and narrative, as well as attunement of the Hizir and Musa narrative with other tellings of this narrative in earlier lessons. In episode 6, there is intra-lesson attunement in the elucidation of "inspiration" with the elucidation of the murshid as "intermediary" from earlier episodes. And in episode 4, where Baba humorously noted that Baba Bayram had assigned him the misfortune that was me, I am defined in the ritual Bektashi way of entry through sponsorship by another baba.

Thus the forms of attunement in these episodes were both memorable and specifically Bektashi, and my affirmations in aphoristic form reflect my attempt at an appropriate "Bektashi reach."

Pattern and Pivot of Later Episodes

in which heretofore ignored narrative episodes are studied for their patterns, and for how they reassert the more customary interaction of Baba and student after the tumult of the earlier episodes

In the earliest discussion of internal bracketing of the Hizir lesson, I noted a major discontinuity between the seventh and eighth episodes. This discontinuity was signaled by a prominent closing in which four "işte"s figured. The episodes before this line, which account for sixty minutes of the seventy-minute whole, have been the focus of attention thus far. The episode that I fully transcribed, translated, and looked at in detail was from this group, as were the openings and closings recently discussed. The episodes after the seventh episode and its line of four "işte"s differ from earlier episodes in that they have a unity of narrative reference. It is to these episodes that I now turn.

PATTERNS ACROSS THE NARRATIVE EPISODES

The most obvious difference between the last set of episodes and the earlier ones is the common reference of the last episodes to Baba Bayram. Baba Bayram, as you may recall from my narrative on how I came to study at the tekke and Baba's affirmation of that narrative (episode 4), was the one who first suggested that I study with Baba.

Baba Bayram was the cook at the Michigan tekke until his death in 1973. His name, which translates as "Father Holiday," suited him. He was short, and had a long white beard. I remember him best with a white apron wrapped around his generous middle, cooking some Middle Eastern specialty like imam bayıldı (a sort of eggplant lasagna whose name, "the imam fainted," refers to the imam fainting either because the dish was so delicious or because the eggplant in the dish soaked up a year's worth of olive oil). He and Baba were both Albanian Bektashis who had ended up at the Bektashi tekke in Egypt in the middle of this century. There they became fast friends, and after the tekke was established in America, Baba invited Baba Bayram to leave Egypt and come to Michigan. Once here, it was Baba Bayram who, although he was not educated in the Ottoman scholarly way Baba Rexheb was, encouraged Baba to write his major book on Bektashism and Islamic mysticism (1970).

In the Hizir Lesson, the last episodes not only refer to Baba Bayram, they also refer chronologically to his life. Illustrating this are my eliciting references in the opening of each of the last episodes:

episode 8
> oh who was Baba Bayram's murshid Baba?

episode 9
> and how long did he {Baba Bayram} stay
> at the tekke {in Albania} Baba?

episode 10
> AND in Egypt~
> you must have found yourself with Baba Bayram~

episode 11
> ehh\
> . WHEN did he {Baba Bayram} become a baba~

This unity of reference and chronological sequence suggest the possibility that this sequence be treated as one episode. However, like the earlier episodes, these interactions also include closing sequences of "işte" phrases, and affirmations and confirmations. On this basis, and on the pull of the earlier pattern, I maintain that these are separate episodes. But as episodes they differ from the earlier ones in several ways.

First, the narrative episodes lack the hedging that was so apparent at the outset of most of the earlier episodes. This leads to a smoother transition between episodes. Second, although in the earlier episodes there was reference to a multitude of topics, including most prominently the murshid and my dissertation, in the latter set of episodes the reference is to Baba Bayram or an aspect of his life. Third, whereas there were several reference-response sequences within the earlier episodes, in the later ones, Baba recounts without uninterruption. I tell no stories and make no aphoristic statements. Except for "yes"s and "um-hmm"s, my talk occurs at the edges. And yet there are interesting patterns across the episodes and within them.

Looking first at episode structure across the narrative episodes, as in the earlier episodes, it is Baba who initiates closure. But what do the episodes enclose?

In terms of Baba Bayram's life, the first of the narrative episodes includes his becoming a *muhib*, that is, a "spiritual member" (the first in a series of vows and ceremonies of the Bektashis), and his repeated acknowledgment of these vows after his military service. The second narrative episode includes his becoming a dervish (the second of the vows and ceremonies of the Bektashis). The third episode relates to Baba's relationship with Baba Bayram in Egypt and in America. And the last episode refers to Baba Bayram's taking his last vows as baba and halife (again, special ceremonies of the Bektashi).

The sequence of muhib-dervish-baba-halife, the ceremonial hierarchy of Bektashi clerics, is thus recounted. That segments in a Bektashi baba's life should break at these divisions is not remarkable. But what is notable is that it is I who ask the last question about Baba Bayram's becoming a baba. Baba had closed the immediately preceding episode by saying that Baba Bayram had stayed in America twelve years. This was said as a cap to his life here, implying his death. And yet the last stage of becoming a baba and halife had not been discussed. Thus my last opening shows attunement to completing the pattern of the Bektashi hierarchy.

Besides the hierarchical pattern, there is also a basic narrative pattern that can be seen within the episodes. It is especially clear in the eighth episode, which is the first narrative episode. This episode began:

```
FT:    eyyy
       hey this Baba Bayram~
       do you remember\ his~
       we should [know his life story {archaic phrase}
       too
Baba:             [know-
FT:    oh who was Baba Bayram's murshid Baba?
```

This last question is akin to asking, "Who brought Baba Bayram into the family of Bektashis?" In Albanian and much Middle Eastern society, the family name has often been derived from the name of the village or town that the family came from. This is true of many babas. But the next identity frame among Bektashis is the name of one's murshid. Thus, in the above question, I show attunement to the Bektashi identity frame.

Baba responded to my question on Baba Bayram's murshid by telling me about this murshid. He then moved from details of the murshid's con-

temporaries in nineteenth-century Albania to describing the poverty of
their tekke, and then on to an account of Baba Bayram being called up for
Ottoman military service. It seems that Baba Bayram's murshid told him
not to go into the military, that the tekke would pay the money required
for exemption. But Baba Bayram insisted on going. His murshid then
remarked:

> ahhh\
> it seems that perhaps ah~
> you regret moving toward being a dervish\
> through this opportunity you want to "unbind" yourself\
> {from the vows}

To this Baba Bayram responded:

> as for that~
> time will show

And sure enough, after serving in the military, Baba Bayram returned and
immediately went to the tekke, where he renewed his vows and remained
there.

In initiating closure of the episode, Baba then noted:

> Baba: it means~
> .. what he wanted (to say) that
> now you understand that I~
> I had given my word to become a dervish~
> not that ah- an excuse~
> that I find an excuse to get out
> of the situation\

I then affirmed the closing and my understanding, both of which Baba
confirmed:

> FT: .... thus~
> ah this showed Baba Bayram's
> ... ess- it showed his essence\
> Baba: yaa\

The pattern that I want to highlight here is Baba Bayram's giving his word ("time will show") and then vindicating it. In examining narrative lessons from the two-year period of taping, I found this to be a basic pattern—that there is a "word," and the narrative is the spinning out of the vindication of that "word." This recurrent theme reflects the important Albanian notion of *bese*, standing by one's word, that underlies the Albanian sense of honor. This pattern became clear to me when I compared different narrative lessons with the same referent. Additional anecdotes always had two parts: someone's "word" and a vindication.

In the above episode, the anecdote on Baba Bayram's military service showed his character and his will to stand by his word. My affirmation,

.... thus~
ah this showed Baba Bayram's
... ess- it showed his essence\

shows my clear attunement with this pattern.

But there is another sort of word-and-vindication pattern that in Sufi lore is even more basic than the foregoing example. This is where the vindication is not of the word-giver's honor, but rather of his or her supernatural connections. This pattern is exemplified in the story of Hizir and Musa.

At the beginning of the story, Musa went to Hizir to be his talib. But Hizir, the prototypical murshid, immediately announced that it would not work, that Musa would not be able to trust him. Musa insisted, and finally Hizir relented on the condition that Musa never question his actions.

The story involves the playing out of three incidents in which each time Musa cannot contain himself and questions Hizir's actions. This clearly shows that, as Hizir had earlier announced, Musa was unable to trust and be patient with Hizir. Thus the murshid's word is vindicated, only here it is not a question of Hizir's character, as it was with Baba Bayram. Rather here the vindication is of Hizir's special sight. Those who have cleansed themselves of the world are able, in Bektashi terms, "to see from behind." They can see the future the way ordinary people can only view the past. Hizir is of this sort, and so vindication of his word vindicates his status as one with this sight—with supernatural connections.

A common "word and vindication" of this sort occurs when a Bektashi baba prays for the birth of a child and then a child is born. Baba's murshid's murshid was not only prayed for before his birth, he was also promised to the Bektashis. Thus, both his very birth and his later becoming a muhib, a dervish, a baba, and a halife vindicated the "word" of the Baba spoken before his birth.

Baba Rexheb was also prayed for before he was born. His murshid's murshid prayed that a boy be born, named him, and also gave him what would be his pen name. He, too, was promised to the Bektashis. Thus Baba's birth, his writing of poetry, and his becoming a muhib, a dervish, a baba and a halife are all vindications of the word of his murshid's murshid. His life is understood in this basic narrative pattern as well as in the Bektashi clerical pattern.

Finally, nefes can be related to this narrative pattern of "word plus vindication." Instead of being separate, however, in a nefes the word is the vindication. As Baba explained in the sixth episode when talking about inspiration, a spiritual poet only writes what he or she receives. The baba who did not write poetry said it was not his fault: he had received nothing through his murshid (dead or living). So when one writes nefes, that is evidence that one is receiving from one's murshid.

An understanding of a unity of word and vindication has also been used in the Islamic community as an argument for the divine nature of the Qur'an. The language of the Qur'an is surpassingly beautiful. Because God is the Creator of the world and its beauty, "words" that are most beautiful can only come from God.

PIVOT OF THE LESSON

In the previous section I noted two important Bektashi rhetorical patterns that were realized in the narrative episodes of the Hizir lesson. These were the chain of hierarchical progression from muhib to dervish to baba to halife, and the narrative pattern of the word and its vindication. I also described how the narrative episodes (8–11) were different from the earlier episodes (1–7) in the lesson. But what of the transition from the earlier episodes to the narrative episodes? Why the shift of the later episodes to narrative style and reference to Baba Bayram? Or more fundamentally, how do the narrative episodes fit in with the overall interaction of the lesson?

The only way to understand the transition to narrative episodes is to look backward, for if the extended talk on Baba Bayram is a response to something, then this something occurred before it in the lesson. In Goffman's deconstruction of the adjacency pair approach to looking at conversation (Sacks, Schegloff, and Jefferson, 1974), he too recommends "a backward look to the structuring of talk" (Goffman, 1981).

What preceded the narrative episodes in the Hizir Lesson was the closing of the seventh episode. This included Baba initiating closure with an "işte" phrase, my affirmation, Baba's confirmation, and our laughter.

End of Episode 7 and Opening of Episode 8

Baba: as for you you listen\   **{initiation of closure}**
             it stays in your memory~
             then what~
                                                       {lower pitch voice}
                     if there are books too~
                     you look in the book how~ (it goes)
             thus it is\

FT: ehhh {accord}   **{affirmation}**
             ... thus it is good Baba\
             .. ehh
             . eyyyy
             .. ey what a good lesson you have given
             today [Baba

Baba: **[eh well what can I do so   {confirmation}**
             .. as for you~ you are left over from Baba Bayram

FT: laughter
Baba: laughter
FT: ey Baba\
Baba and FT: {continued laughter}

FT: eyyy   **{opening of episode 8}**
             hey this Baba Bayram~
             do you remember\ his~
             we should [know his life story {archaic phrase}
             too
Baba: [know-
FT: oh who was Baba Bayram's murshid Baba?

It is Baba's confirmation (all in boldface) that I will concentrate on, for I see it as a pivotal utterance of the lesson and as a remarkable example of Baba's way of teaching. The confirmation was in response to my affirmation that ended with my thanking Baba for the good lesson he had given that day. The confirmation can thus be understood as a sort of mediation of this thanking:

Baba: eh well what can I do so
        .. as for you~ you are left over from Baba Bayram\

Baba's reference to Baba Bayram here is especially significant. The only other time we had spoken of Baba Bayram in the lesson was twenty minutes earlier in the fourth episode when I had been telling my narrative of how I came to study with Baba. Baba Bayram had been the one to suggest I study with him. Baba's affirmation there helped bring shape and closure to my narrative as well as humor:

Baba: anlaşılan Baba Bayram havale etti "bela" bana

* * * * *

Baba: so it's to be understood that Baba Bayram
        assigned to me this "misfortune"

Thus Baba's referral to Baba Bayram in his confirmation at the close of the seventh episode had resonance to his earlier affirmation in the fourth episode and our pleasure there. This intra-lesson attunement brought a certain cohesion to the lesson. At the same time, Baba's confirmation with its reference to my "Bektashi entry" to study with him has ritual parallels that go beyond the lesson.

In the ceremony of initiation a talib needs a *rehber* to set one on the spiritual way, and a murshid to guide one on that way. When Baba Bayram was in Egypt, he had hoped Baba Rexheb would remain there with him so that together they could be the rehber and murshid for the Egyptian tekke. Thus Baba's reference to Baba Bayram having assigned me to him has ritual as well as humorous resonance.

In initiating the eighth episode, I picked up on Baba's reference to Baba Bayram. I read this new focus on the agent of my study with Baba as a way of reinforcing Baba's and my relationship within a Bektashi frame.

But why then, after such a long lesson, did our relationship need to be reinforced in this Bektashi frame? Again, because my reference to Baba Bayram is a response, we need to look backward to what came before. The four "işte"s are a clue that something unusual transpired in the episode of which they are the terminal bracket. It is here I find what for me was the low point of the whole lesson.

The episode that contains the low point is the seventh episode. The episode before that was the one in which we had been talking about inspiration in poetry. I had felt that I was following and understanding well. Then at the outset of the seventh episode, I had asked if inspiration in music were similar to inspiration in poetry. Baba had responded with a couplet from a poem by Nesimi (fifteenth century).

.. bu muzikiden ey sami~
sana gel nesne keşve oldu~

makamatın beyan eyle~
usulun göster *edvarın*

* * * * *

.. O listener from this music
come let's see what it reveals in you

it makes clear your *tune*
your *rhythm* and shows your *mode*

In the last two lines, all the italicized words have multiple meanings, both musical and mystic. *Makamat* signifies not only "tune," but also "place" and "spiritual stage." The word I translated as "rhythm" has a more general meaning of "style" or "manner"; and the last word, which I translated as "mode," more generally refers to "cycles," or "duties," which also implies "duties commanded by God."

After reciting the couplet, Baba added that he had learned this nefes from his murshid, Selim Baba. Then he went on to explain the couplet, and at the end of his explanation he initiated closure with the first "işte." But I was unable to follow part of Baba's explanation of the couplet, so instead of affirming his initiation of closure, I asked for a fuller explanation of what I thought was confusing me. In particular, I asked about the last word of the couplet, *edvar*, which is the plural of *devir* and usually signifies "cycle." Baba explained again. Still I did not understand. Then Baba said:

po görmeden anlayamazsın tabii\

* * * * *

well without seeing of course you can't understand\

This was a blow to me, for I interpreted "to see" in the mystic sense of experiencing things. Baba then told me to open the dictionary to the word *devir*. I refused, telling him I knew that it meant "cycle" or "duty," but perhaps I did not know what it meant in musical terms.

In a later lesson, I learned that my confusion with Baba's explanation was a classic problem of frame. Ottoman poetry was visual as well as auditory. Just as calligraphy was an esteemed art form in Islamic society, similarly the way a poem looked on the paper was also art, even to the point of there being "visual rhyme," in which the Arabic consonants and long vowels looked similar but their pronunciation in particular words did not rhyme (Andrews, 1976).

In the case of Baba's experience with the couplet by Nesimi, the reference to cycles or modes had been picked up and played out in the actual writing of the poem such that the whole poem was written in circles. (This is also done with prayers, in which the first word is in the center, and then the prayer circles round and round, just as pilgrims circle the Ka'aba in Mecca.) When Baba had been describing these circles on the page, I had been trying to relate them to the more restricted sense of cycles in the poem. And when he had said that I could not understand without seeing, he had literally meant seeing the page. But assuming that it was the multiple meanings and perhaps musical understanding that eluded me, I persevered, and Baba dutifully explained the musical explanations of the words. I suggested I understood, but Baba knew better and repeated his explanation, which he then capped with the second closure and "işte" phrase.

Yet again, I withheld affirmation, and with a shift of focus asked Baba the words that were presented in the Prologue:

. haaa bu severim baba~

　　　　　　　　　　　　　a- anlamak~
nasıl öğretti Selim Baba sana\　　　　{with frustration}

* * * * *

. haaa this I would like Baba~

                                t- to understand~
    how did Selim Baba teach you\   {with frustration}

Notice the hedging, and although it is not as apparent in the English, the Turkish syntax is loose and highly dialectal (subject and indirect object follow the verb).

   As noted earlier in the Prologue, my question on how Selim Baba had taught Baba was not an innocent question. In one sense this question was an attempt to short-circuit the couplet by Nesimi and Baba's explanation that I could not follow. In referring back to Selim Baba I was referring back to the person who had taught Baba the couplet, as if I could thereby ignore the couplet. But I was also crying out, for why after so many years couldn't I understand these poems! Baba responded to this cry with a remedy, which I then repeatedly acknowledged with laughter, "yes"s, and an affirmation.

FT: . haaa this I would like Baba~

                                    t- to understand~
       how did Selim Baba teach you\
Baba: . thus by listening~
FT: by listening~
Baba: yaa\
FT: {laughs}
Baba: -like you~
       how~
       so much~
       . . . so many things you have learned from me~
FT: yes
                                         {softly}

Baba: but how have you learned~
       by listening\
FT: it's true
Baba: I make friendly talk~
       I speak~
FT: yes
Baba: as for you you listen\
       it stays in your memory~
       then what~

```
         if there are books too~    (lower pitch)
         you look in the book how~ (it goes)
         thus it is\
FT:                  ehh {accord}
         ... thus it is good Baba\
         .. ehh
         . eyyy
         .. ey what a good lesson you have given
         today [Baba
Baba:        [eh well what can I do so
         .. as for you~ you are left over from Baba Bayram\
```

Baba's first response to my question about how Selim Baba taught him reflected his understanding of the reach of my question. Instead of describing how his teacher taught him, Baba referred instead to how he learned. At a deeper level this is what I was asking, for I wanted to know if there was something I was doing wrong that caused me not to follow the nefes. Baba responded further to this worry of mine by stating that I had learned much from him. His response is a remedy, because it responds to my sense of myself that has taken a beating from not being able to understand his explanation. This remedy reassured me that I was not a dolt in Baba's eyes. Baba then moved for a third time toward closure, with a third "işte" phrase.

The fourth "işte" is mine, when in the affirmation I mirror Baba's *işte boyle* (thus it is this way) with my *işte güzel* (thus it is good). This affirmation, after three tries on Baba's part, shows the sufficiency of his remedy. Baba's ensuing confirmation, of my being left over from Baba Bayram, reinforces his remedy. In referring to my Bektashi entry, Baba also asserts my legitimacy in a Bektashi way in the enterprise that is our interaction.

That I then picked up on Baba's reference to Baba Bayram can be seen as a sort of echo of Baba's reinforcement of his remedy. Notice though that all reference to the project of the dissertation has long since evaporated, as has the quasi-interview format in which I earlier asked so many questions. Instead, in the last narrative episodes, we have returned to a less risky, more familiar balance of interaction in which Baba does most of the talking, and as he suggested, I listen. Thus we have adjusted back, and in this process of attunement, reasserted at the same time our relationship and our usual way of interacting.

III. Keying Interaction with Baba

In the last chapter I explored internal bracketing of the Hizir lesson. This led to a definition of episoding across the lesson, a description of episode structure, and an interpretation of the major shift in the last part of the lesson. Attunement of my language and Baba's was brought out in the sequences of remedy and mediation within episodes, in the affirmations and confirmations that closed episodes, and in the shift near the end of the lesson.

In this chapter I adopt a different perspective. Instead of comparing structures across the lesson I look at an overall message that can be gleaned from "keyings" of the interaction of talib and murshid throughout the lesson. By "keying" I refer to "systematic signaling of how an activity is to be interpreted in terms of another known frame." Gregory Bateson's example of monkeys "keying" that they were playing, to indicate "this is not fight," is a basic illustration of keying (Bateson, 1972; Goffman, 1974). An advantage of looking at keyings is that they relate particular patterns of interaction (the signals of the transformation of the frame) to socially recognizable activities.

The particular keying of the interaction that I evolve is "this is not a joust." Like many keyings as well as many Sufi anecdotes, this is a negative definition. Attunement here is brought out not as a changing progression toward a shared form, but rather as an uncovering of recurrent messages of interaction.

Preliminary to Keying: "Knowing of His Not Knowing"

> in which the student or talib is revealed as one of patent insecurity, who by fostered default learns dependence on the murshid

There is a poetic series of linked adages that Baba has on occasion recited in Arabic.[1] Regretfully I do not recall the contexts of recitation.

> Knowing not,
> And knowing naught of his not knowing,
> He scatters.
> Hasten from him.
>
> Knowing not,
> Yet knowing of his not knowing,
> He seeks.
> Teach him.
>
> Knowing,
> Yet knowing naught of his knowing,
> He sleeps.
> Wake him.
>
> Knowing,
> And knowing of his knowing,
> He centers.
> Draw near him.

In the second stanza, the line I translated as "he seeks" is in Arabic the nominal "talib."

This extended adage asserts that a talib is one who "knows that he or she does not know." That which he or she does not know, refers of course to more than facts, for when Baba and the Sufis in general speak of knowledge, they mean spiritual knowledge—experience in coming closer to God. More generally, though, "knowing of one's not knowing" refers to an acknowledgment that one is unable to predict sequences and find meaning within a new situation. It is the limbo and anomie of foreigners who finally realize their frames of expectation do not fit. They drift and stumble. This is a common experience in cross-cultural study, except for those who carry their empire within—thinking either that all the world should emulate them, or, more insidiously, that at base all the world is already like them. In other words, "knowing of one's not knowing" is a sort of suspension of frame.

In my case of studying with Baba, the suspension of frame was especially intense. As a university student part of my identity was wrapped up in what it meant to be a student and to study. There was strong pressure to apply my frame of how one studies and learns to studying with Baba. When this frame was contradicted, I was at a loss.

The major contradiction was my notion of how the teacher should behave compared with how Baba did behave. My expectations were that the teacher would overtly direct the flow of information and evaluation of the student's learning. That is, there should be topics, and Baba as the teacher should set them. He should be overtly in charge. He should speak first; but he did not. Thus when I had to begin the sessions, when it was I who had to open talk after episode breaks, I felt in a cross-cultural double bind. Baba would not begin, so clearly I had to. Yet to do so set me up in my mind as in charge, though I knew I was not.

Part of my problem was a foggy sense of knowledge as information and as separable from the student, and of knowing as a passive state. This leads to a view of learning as "a banking enterprise," to use Paulo Freire's term. Maturana and Varela (1987) claim that this view of knowledge and of knowing is a common fallacy. Rather, according to them, every act of knowing brings forth a world; all knowing is effective action. This view squares well with the Sufi vision of spiritual knowing as the action of drawing closer to God. For the lowly talib however, what is lacking is a frame for understanding what is going on. For me this was manifested in the feeling that there was no syllabus.

In my interaction with Baba, this lack of frame, this "not knowing," was reflected in features often characterized as features of "negative politeness" (Brown and Levinson, 1987), namely, hedging, pausing, faltering syntax, distractions to the tape-recorder, and prolonged development. For example, the fourth episode began:

```
FT:    .. you know~
       .. hey let's have a look\
{checks tape-recorder}
           as for me what I like are stories\
                              . one thing I like
       -is stories\
Baba:                    yaa
FT:                          for example Hizir and Musa~
       ex-
Baba:    ya
FT:         -actly a mur-
Baba:                 ex-
```

FT: -shid~
> what he is\
> are there others **Baba**?

Two other common features in such passages are my ubiquitous calling out to Baba, as in bold above, and instances of my moving into his dialect. (These include unrounding of front vowels, fossilizing of suffixes usually governed by vowel harmony, and substitution of locative for dative postpositions.) Both my calling out to Baba and my use of his dialect can be classified as features of "positive politeness."

The deferential strategies of both "negative politeness" and "positive politeness" by the same person in an exchange are sometimes interpreted as an attempt both to maintain social distance and to reduce social distance. Here, though, this analysis falls short of explaining my behavior. Rather I interpret this mixture of moves as reflecting not just questions of deference toward Baba but also questions of my own demeanor,[2] of how I relate to myself in a situation where I am profoundly unsure.

My uncertainly stems from several areas: what to talk about, how to put it, my place in initiating talk, and where the lessons are going. These would be concerns of any talib. Compounding this unsureness is isolation. Certainly one way in which we anchor our sense of frames of meaning of the world is through multiple messages that reinforce our contentions (Goffman, 1974). But the situation of the talib seeking to learn from the murshid is that only through the murshid is there light. In the case where there is only one line of validation of a frame, we are on a slender line indeed. As Baba chants in the nefes from Pir Sultan Abdal (sixteenth century):

> Derdim çoktur kangisine yanayim   hu
> > Yine tazelendi yürek yaresi
> Ben bu derde kande derman bulayim   hu
> > **Meğer Şah elinden ola çaresi**   hu

* * * * *

> So many are my sufferings, which shall consume me   hu
> > The wounds of my heart again are raw.
> For my sufferings, where shall I find remedy,   hu
> > **If there be cure only from the hand of the Shah.**   hu

Quatrains from nefes like this one have much accumulated resonance, but here notice the last line. As Baba once explained, "Shah" can stand for the murshid. There is a strong understanding that any assistance can come only from the murshid. Also, the "hu" at the end of the lines, as explained in the first chapter, comes from the Arabic for "he" and can refer to God or to one's murshid through whom God is invoked. Thus "hu" is like my saying "Baba," a calling out to the murshid.

If the Bektashi tradition expects and promotes the suspension of frame of the talib, the sense of "knowing of one's not knowing," what is the point of this experience? Another name for suspension of frame is "negative experience." Goffman has noted that there are uses of negative experience (1974). Short suspensions, like some laughter, allow closer reintegration to the previous frame, but longer negative experiences allow reintegration into some other frame.

Death is a major frame break for most of us. Among the Bektashis, as with many other mystics, there is an understanding expressed by the Arabic phrase *mauta qabla en ta mouta*, or "death before dying." It involves a dying to this world and its values, a cleansing so that only God lives inside one. That is the goal. But the way is understood through the murshid, who both promotes the negative experience and serves as the only way to a reintegration. Thus the "knowing of one's not knowing" cuts one loose and focuses trust on the murshid. My calling out to Baba and my use of his dialect also reflect this movement toward dependence on him.

The Keying: "This Is Not a Joust"

> in which Baba's consumate skill in verbal jousting is portrayed, his utter restraint from jousting behavior with the talib is described, and the ever-present binding of murshid and talib is revealed

The suspension of frame of the talib and the resulting insecurity and dependence on the murshid set up a keying of the talib-murshid relationship that I refer to as "this is not a joust." In this situation the talib knows he or she could be easily shamed or bested by the murshid, and yet the murshid does not do this. The talib's sense of the murshid's restraint further strengthens the bond of talib and murshid. But why should the thought of being verbally bested occur to a talib?

Verbal Jousts Among Albanian Bektashis: Baba's Skill in Swift Rejoinder

In the Middle East and Balkans, and in the Albanian Bektashi community in America, people talk a lot. They sit on porches and benches outside, in coffeehouses and restaurants inside, or just around the table at home and eat and drink and talk. In coffeehouses the men also play cards and backgammon, but still there is much talk. The women, too, share the pleasure of talking, which is facilitated by the telephone. News travels with remarkable speed. In recognition of this, there is never formal publicity on the local level for the constantly rotating lunar-based holidays or individual ceremonies at the tekke. People simply get word.

Speaking and using language well are also highly valued. Eulogies by men are an important part of memorial ceremonies. Good singers are renowned throughout the community. And poetry is esteemed, be it in the American-Albanian newspaper *Dielli* ("The Sun"), in the privately published collections of poems that are passed around, or at public gatherings. When poetry is declaimed, people listen. Furthermore, recognition of speaking well is not limited to special occasions. Any gathering provides a potential audience for skill in repartee. The tekke's basement kitchen, with its long table well-suited for bringing people together, its ready pot for brewing coffee, and its closeness to the back door for welcoming newcomers, is the frequent scene of verbal duels. One warm September day a short joust took place there, after a lunch of chicken, potatoes, eggplant, salad, and bread.

The dessert that day was melon from the tekke garden, served with white cheese. As I moved Baba's plate of melon in front of him, he asked in Turkish for the *çatal*, the fork to my left. It had been used, however, so I rose to get a clean one. The dervish on the other side of the table, the side closer to the drawers, saw me rise and asked in Albanian, "Pirun?" I paused. I was unsure of the Albanian for "fork." Then I nodded as he proceeded to get a clean one from the drawer. I repeated, "Pirun."

Baba, who had observed all this, asked Zoti Ago (pronounced "aa-go" with stress on the first syllable), the tall ninety-year-old Albanian gentleman to his right, what "fork" was in his dialect. (Zoti Ago comes from Labëri, a region in southwestern Albania whose songs sing only of heroes.) Zoti Ago answered, "Sforku." Later I found out that Zoti Ago was playing with us, for people from his region say *pirun*, too, while *sforku* indicates "pitchfork." Then, however, I took him seriously and asked if the word for "spoon" was also different. No, apparently *fuqinë* was *fuqinë*

"But," added Zoti Ago, with a glimmer in his eye, "the Albanian of Labëri is pure, Baba's language is urban and full of Greek."

This pronouncement was a direct challenge, for in Albania one identifies with one's region. As for Baba, he comes from the southern Albanian town of Gjirokastër, which is quite close to the Greek border. This border has been the ground of much contention, with Greece claiming Baba's region as part of Greece (the northern Epirus) and even occupying it early in this century. In this region, differences among people include religion. The Greeks are Orthodox Christian, whereas many Albanians like Baba are Muslim. So when Zoti Ago said that Baba's language was full of Greek, this was a put-down on two counts. First it imputed that Baba was less than Zoti Ago in terms of being Albanian, and second, by association, that Baba was less Muslim.

In responding to the challenge, Baba was hampered in that his dialect is indeed full of Greek. But that did not stop him from overcoming Ago. Ago put forth his challenge in Albanian while looking at me, for surely I was the audience of this duel:

Ago: the language of Labëri is pure~
      Baba's language is urban and full of Greek\

Baba turned to me to respond:

Baba: kâfirin mali helal\

I gasped with pleasure! The swiftness of reframing in Baba's response caught me off guard.

To share appreciation of Baba's response, it is the reframing that I must elucidate, but first I will translate. The first word of Baba's response, *kâfir*, means "unbeliever" or "non-Muslim." Here, of course, "unbeliever" refers to the Christian Greeks. The second word of Baba's response, *mali*, means "property of." Thus *kâfirin mali* refers to "the property of the unbelievers." In the context of Ago's challenge the reference is to the Greek language. The third and last word of Baba's response is *helal*, an Arabic term which signifies that something is "permitted by religious law." Thus Baba's *kâfirin mali helal* could be translated as "the property of the unbelievers is permitted." But the further, deeper meaning of Baba's response lies in the reframing.

In his terse response, Baba had reframed "the language of the Christian Greeks," which was imputed to be contaminating his, from "the language of an enemy" and on a par with one's own, to "a property of unbelievers"—something of decidedly inferior status. Most important though, this shift set up Baba and the Albanians of his region as military victors, who, in appropriating something of the Greeks, were merely taking their due in the spoils of war.

Baba explained in Albanian to the others at the table what he had said to me in Turkish. Then he turned to me and asked, "But do you know where this [saying] comes from?"

I replied that the distinction between what is *helal* or "permitted," and *haram* or "forbidden," comes from the Qur'an. "Yes, but there is more," responded Baba.

He then explained that the line *kafirin mali helal* is a quotation from Hafiz, one of the greatest Persian poets of all time. It seems that Hafiz, a fourteenth-century poet, was called to task for taking a line from Yazid, a poet of the eighthth century. Like Baba, Hafiz had been challenged in a verbal duel. And like Baba, Hafiz's response was not to deny that he had taken the line, but to recast the line and thereby himself, saying *mali kyafir hestu ber mumin helal*, which in Persian means "the property of unbelievers is permitted." (In this case, although both Hafiz and Yazid, the earlier poet, were Muslims, Yazid was considered an "unbeliever" by Hafiz because Yazid was of the Sunni Umayyad branch of Islam. This branch of Muslims fought against and killed most of Ali's family in the seventh century, which brought them the undying enmity of all Shi'a Muslims, who greatly esteem Ali's family. Hafiz and those around him were considered in sympathy with the Shi'a.)

"That means," I said to Baba, "that there is a lot of Greek in your dialect." "Yes," said Baba. Zoti Ago nodded. But it also meant that Baba had met and overcome the verbal challenge and overcome it in style, by reaching back six centuries in the tradition of such jousts.

Such are the capabilities of Baba in the kitchen arena. As the quotation Baba selected shows, the tradition of verbal jousting extends back in time. In the past, this tradition included the more restricted and dramatic duels between poets in which the loser was killed. But dignity and esteem are no small spoil, either.

Another example of verbal jousts among Bektashis is the following pair of couplets. Baba first recited these to me in the basement kitchen in my early years of study with him. Interestingly enough, both Baba and I made reference to them in the Hizir lesson, but here I will elucidate them only in terms of their representing a joust.

Sualim var size Recep Effendi.
Ali Tanrı mıdır Tanrı değil mi?

Sual etti bana sırrı kadimi:
Acep kâfir midir, kâfir değil mi.

＊ ＊ ＊ ＊ ＊

I have a question for you, Master Rejep.
Is Ali God or is he not?

He has asked me the ancient secret:
I wonder, is he an unbeliever, or is he not.

The first couplet represents the challenge. The one challenged, Master Rejep, is addressed by formal title and in the formal second person pronominal. The question itself, however, is an invitation to admission of heresy.

The "Ali" referred to is the son-in-law of the Prophet Muhammad and the one to whom Sufis attribute the revelation of mystic understanding of the Qur'an. They therefore regard him highly. In Ottoman times, though, to state publicly one's regard for Ali could bring the wrath of the Ottoman rulers, who were Sunni Muslims and who often associated regard for Ali with loyalty to their enemy the Shi'a Persians. Further, Islam in general is stringently monotheistic, so a positive answer to the question would certainly be blasphemous, and perhaps traitorous. (The challenger kept himself somewhat distant from the dangers of his question by using for God an old Turkish word, *Tanrı*, thus avoiding "Allah" and its Qur'anic association.)

In the second couplet, Master Rejep meets this challenge first by sidestepping the direct exchange by employing the third person ("he has asked me"). Then, instead of answering the question, Master Rejep reveals the intent of the questioner—to trap him in heresy.

Baba's enjoyment of this exchange, besides the banter, focuses on the ability of Master Rejep to match in his response the rhythm and syntactic pattern of the challenge. This crafted reach to the language of the challenger is attunement as one-upmanship.[3]

TRANSFORMATION OF SWIFT REJOINDER

The verbal jousts described above can be seen as "keyed to" or "patterned on" warfare. Historically, the relationship between verbal play and warfare may sometimes have been even closer in that some warfare may have been a response to failed verbal play, or to verbal play that was too successful. With the talib, though, the situation is quite different. There, I contend, the skills of the murshid are muted and transformed. This is nowhere clearer than when the talib makes blatant errors that almost invite swift rejoinders.

For example, at the outset of the Hizir lesson, I made a blatant error of attribution. The error occurred after Baba's response to my halting outset and question on the relationship of murshid and talib.

8. Baba: between the murshid~
and talib~
there is a very close tie
9. FT: yes
10. Baba: . such that even~
it has been said
in the words of the esteemed ones~ {*kaulu kibar*}
{below in Arabic}

el-murshidu fi talibihi~
qe nabihu fi ummetihi
. that is~
. a- the bond~
. between talib and murshid~
resembles that bond~
of the Prophet and his community\
11. FT: hmm

My response to this quotation and translation was to ask where the quotation came from. When Baba had introduced the adage, however, he had already attributed it to *kaulu kibar*, an Arabic phrase that can be translated as "words of the great or esteemed ones." So when I asked my question, Baba repeated what he had said—*kaulu kibar*—which he then translated into the Turkish—*büyükler söylemişler*, with similar meaning. To this I asked:

15. FT: haa\
that means that in the Prophet's~
in the time of the Prophet~
from among his friends? (it was said)

It is totally improbable that people in the time of the Prophet Muhammad (seventh century) would have said that the "murshid is to the talib as the Prophet to his community." It is improbable because Sufi murshids only gained prominence in Islam beginning in the tenth century. Instead the adage that Baba recited can be seen as a legitimizing ploy in which a later relationship, not sanctioned by Orthodox Islam, seeks legitimacy by being related to one of the basic relationships of Islam—that of Muhammad and his community.

My confusion, however, was with another Arabic phrase, *ashab an-nabi*, or the "companions of the Prophet," which did imply people at the time of the Prophet. Thoughtlessly I interchanged this with *kaulu kibar*. Baba's immediate response was not to call attention to my error at all. Rather he picked up on the last word of my question:

16. Baba: from the friends\
      from the great ones\
      they are to have said that\

Friends can be construed ahistorically.

Baba did correct my error, although the correction came several minutes and forty turns later. It is this sort of subtlety that conversational researchers who confine themselves to short exchanges may miss.[4]

The context of correction was Baba's explanation of the difference in the relationship between God and human beings in Sunni Islam and in the Sufi Orders. Baba made the point that in the Orders this relationship was not conceived of as direct from human to God, but through an intermediary. This relationship has been referred to before in this book, but here it is the attribution of the adage that is important:

64. Baba: especially
      in Bektashism~
      it is not like that\
      "these ones" say
             .. a- .... the murshid~
             .. is to the talib~
             .. as the Prophet~
             . is to the community

Baba had given this same adage at the outset of the lesson. This time he did not state it first in Arabic as before, however, but stated it directly in Turkish. And more important, he also added the attribution that the adage was said by Bektashis.

Baba's talk here constitutes a correction of my earlier error. The correction is accomplished through a recontextualization of the adage in which the Arabic is forgotten and the attribution made specific. This format differs utterly from the swift rejoinder of the joust in its timing and interactional impact. It is gentler yet than a self-correction, and I am free to feel not-corrected, only enriched. (I discovered this correction only upon reading the transcription of the lesson, not during the lesson itself.)

Another example of Baba correcting me was in the fourth episode of the Hizir lesson when I asked for more stories like that of Hizir and Musa. This episode has been discussed, but here I would like to emphasize how it differs from the "challenge-rejoinder" format of the jousts.

The reason that asking for more stories was an error, and a grosser mistake than the above confusion in attribution, is that it was a confusion of prerogatives. Baba is the one to call up stories. Without meaning to I had brought up a challenge. Baba's response, instead of asserting his authority, was to deflect me back to the story he had already told and to say that if I explained that story well, half my thesis would be done. I realized I had erred, and fell back on our relationship, saying that I would "go home, reflect, and come back and ask more questions." Baba's following mediation was the antithesis of the blow of the swift rejoinder. He used my first name and stated directly that all was possible for me, and that he wished me to rise high.

It is possible, however, that the previous two examples should not even be considered corrections. In the first example, it may have been chance that the adage was recontextualized and done so with more specific attribution. As for the second example, if "correction" implies "replacement of an error or mistake by what is correct" (Schegloff et al., 1977), then it was not corrected during the stream of interaction of that episode. Baba's response could be seen as potentially initiating repair, but he did not confront me with the matter of usurpation of prerogatives. Indeed, I understood my error only after the lesson, in what must be considered self-correction.

Self-correction is the antithesis of the moves of a joust. In a joust, the purpose is to defeat the other openly, not reform one's self. I see self-correction as the mode of correction in Bektashi teaching. As Baba said, the talib's place is to listen. Thus the confrontation of the talib is played out within him or herself, and as a result the initiation of correction becomes vitally important. As this is a subtler matter than direct confrontation by the murshid, the interaction is raised a level on the scale of careful listening.

In addition to these two examples, there are also less dramatic responses by Baba that border on correction. Here I refer to exchanges like those discussed at the beginning of chapters four and six in which Baba agreed with my points of there being no murshids in America and of there being many murshids in the history of Bektashism; yet he insisted on extending these beyond America and beyond Bektashism. These examples still differ from the joust format in that in a verbal joust, the one challenged seeks not to extend the point of the challenger, but rather to demolish or overcome it.

Another interesting category is violation of interactional conventions, such as when I do not affirm Baba's closure (episode 2). But it is the nature of such conventions that Baba can only draw attention to the violations; the affirmation must come from me.

Finally, Baba's responses to my aphoristic affirmations, like his extensions to my initiations of episodes, border on correction. For example, in the first aphoristic affirmation, I started with "to each talib there should be a murshid," which I then self-corrected to "without a murshid, one sees nothing." Baba's response was three-tiered. First he said, "we say," followed by what is at best a transitional form to what the Bektashis say, but which builds on my words: "He who goes on the way without a murshid is like a ship without a captain." Then Baba added that this was like a car without a driver. In closing, he made a statement closer to a Bektashi form, that "on the spiritual way, a person does not progress without a murshid." The main modification is the addition of "spiritual way." Here again, in contrast to the swift rejoinder, Baba develops the modification over three utterances, while picking up my laughter along the way.

Yet another modification of my formulation occurred after the affirmation of the fourth episode. Here I had stated that "the teacher who truly teaches must be a murshid." Baba agreed, but then insisted that in saying "murshid" I must mean "perfected murshid." To make this point he recited a modified couplet from Niyazi Mısri:

Her mürşide dil verme gıl
yalnız safta öğretir [yolunu sarpa uğradır]

Mürşid-i kâmil olanın
gayet yolu asan imiş

* * * * *

Do not give your heart to each murshid
He may teach only false ways [his way will lead to difficulty]

As for the perfected murshid
His way is said to be truly smooth

This response differs from my formulation in that it states the negative consequences of choosing a bad murshid, and it states them in nefes form. It also differs from a swift rejoinder because Baba situates it as an elucidation of his point on the necessity of a perfected murshid. In fact it reforms my own statement.

In these two examples, Baba's responses resemble what are called "expansions" in child language studies. Expansions occur when a child says something that is perhaps only two words but presumably expresses more, and the mother spins out what a fuller form might be. In comparison with the intent of a swift rejoinder, the purpose of the expansion is not to show the mother's superior powers of expression, although those are incontestable. Rather, the expansion offers a translation to the child in the form confirmed by the society of the mother, and notification that through such formulations one gains entry to that society. I see nefes in that light, as a fuller sort of communication of Bektashis, an attunement that Baba would gently lead me into.

Transformation of Competitive Intent: The Logology of Binding

Instead of using his considerable verbal skills to deliver a blow, Baba used these skills to mediate my errors and affirm our relationship. I see this affirming of our relationship and other relationships as an underlying theme of the whole interaction. In particular, in contrast to the competitive intent of the joust, in the interaction between Baba and myself there is constant reference and action toward binding.

Another way to describe talk about binding is to use Kenneth Burke's coinage and speak of the "logology" of binding. Just as theology can be understood as "words about God," so Burke defines logology as "words about words" (1961). One of the ways Burke develops logologies is through close reading of texts and tracing of key terms. He sees a relation between narrative unfolding and the cyclical recurrence of these key terms. He then relates the narrative unfolding to a growing understanding of these words in a view of language.

In an especially apt example in his *Rhetoric of Religion* (1961), Burke traces closely related words and forms of "to cling" (*inhaerere*) through St. Augustine's *Confessions*. The context is Augustine's relation to God, but the narrative understanding moves from Augustine's relation with his mother and her important role in his eventual conversion, through the relation of Christ clinging to the Word, the heavens clinging to God, and finally to the clinging of every obedient intelligence of the heavenly city to God. Burke then relates the speechless clinging of the infant to the silent verbalizing in the afterlife.

In the Hizir lesson, Baba's first comment was

mürşid ile talib~ arasında~
çok sıkı bir **alaka** var\

* * * * *

between the murshid and his talib~
there is a very close **attachment**\

Baba then went on to describe this "attachment" in terms of the adage in Arabic that "the murshid is to the talib as the Prophet to the community." This presumes familiarity with the Qur'an and Hadith (sayings of the Prophet) in which Muhammad's travail and concern for his community is a frequent topic. In Baba's translation of the above adage from Arabic to Turkish, he used the word *ilişiklik*, or "bond," to describe the relationship of murshid to talib.

As the seventy-minute interaction continued, reference to binding in words, similes, and narratives was various and pervasive. The words include:

alaka ("attachment")
ilişiklik ("bond")
vasita ("intermediary")
tutmak ("to hold")

havale etmek ("to assign")
rabt etmek ("to connect")
irtibat ("connection")
bağlama ("tie")
bağlayış ("tie")

The similes that embody binding are those of the relationship of murshid and talib. And the narratives with reference to binding include that of Hizir and Musa, as well as the episodes on Baba Bayram. These references and embodiments of binding can be categorized, for the purpose of discussion, into three groups: ritual, serial, and personal.

Ritual binding is repeatedly brought up in the lesson. It surfaces in the first episode in the Hizir and Musa narrative, in the fifth episode in a contrast between the practice of an Albanian Orthodox Christian leader and the Bektashis, and finally in the narrative episodes at the end of the lesson in the clerical steps of Baba Bayram. The recurrent reference to ritual binding signals its importance.

In the first episode of the lesson, the ritual aspect is alluded to in the third incident of the narrative on Hizir and Musa. There, Hizir commanded Musa to *hold* onto his collar and to say "Pir Hakk, Pir Hakk" as they swam across the sea. To say "Pir Hakk " in Turkish is to assert that the *pir* or "founder of the Order" is *Hakk*—"the Truth" (God). The murshid is understood as representing the pir, so when the talib says "Pir Hakk" he is directing his prayer to the murshid.

The ritual sense of these actions is undeniable, with the sea as the "unknown" and the journey or spiritual way as possible only by holding closely to the murshid. These understandings point to the initiation ceremony of the Bektashis.

Musa does not do as he is told, however, and so his actions represent a misfiring of the ritual. Instead of calling out to the murshid, he calls out to God, at which point he begins to drown. Baba later explained that Musa's calling out to God when Hizir was already doing that for them both showed separation. To whom should God listen—Musa or Hizir? The point, which was dramatized logologically, was that the way of the talib is only through the murshid. A logolistic understanding of this incident is that here the "word" is essentially a "vow." Hizir commanded certain words of fealty. Musa could not hold to these, at which point he not only started to drown, but was also rejected as a talib of Hizir.

After the narrative, with its negative definition of the talib, Baba moved to a positive definition of the talib with the following statement:

he {talib} must be so enamoured {*sevdalı*}
and so in love {*aşık*} that he
destroy himself for the sake of him {the murshid}

Baba then illustrated this point with the adage that "the talib should be to the murshid as a corpse in the hands of the body-washer." He glossed the adage by saying:

. o kadar teslim olmali talib murşide~
nasıl olu olan adam~
o ki uğdurur oni~
yeykar o ne yapar~
ki hiç bir şey soylemiyor o uli[5]~
oyle olmali da bu\

* * * * *

. the talib must have given himself up
    -so much for the murshid that~
how is the one who is dead~
he who prepares him~
he washes him and whatever he does~
so the dead one says nothing~
so must he {talib} be\

Just as Musa's starting to drown was explained in terms of language, so the loving and self-giving talib's behavior is described in terms of language. In this instance, however, it is silence that functions as the vow in showing devotion.

In addition to the Hizir narrative in the first episode, there were two other places in the course of the lesson that referred to ritual binding. One of these occurred in the fifth lesson, when in building on a contrast that I had made with Christianity and the laying on of hands, Baba observed that a difference between Bektashism and Christianity was that most Christian ceremonies for ordaining clerics were public and there were no *manevi irtibat* (spiritual connectings) as in the Bektashi ceremonies.

The second instance is when Baba refers to ritual binding in the last episodes. There, Baba Bayram renewed his declarations to remain in the tekke after his military service, and he subsequently became a dervish and then a baba. Still another reference to ritual binding in the last episodes is Baba's remark that in his plans to come to America he would stay with friends, but he could not work because of his garb.

> I will go to America\
> there is no other way\
> . they~ there are people I know there~
> eh~ . and there~
> I will stay with them\
> as for myself~ . I cannot work
> because of my garb {*elbisem var*}

When he became a Bektashi dervish in 1922, Baba had put on special clothes: a *hırka*, or long sleeveless vest that is associated with Muhammad's heavenly journey in which he encountered Ali, the revealer of mystical understanding of the Qur'an, already in heaven; a *taç*, or headpiece that covers his head just as the *hırka* covers the body; and a *kemer*, or belt associated with yet another ceremony in which Baba committed himself to celibacy. Like the words Hizir told Musa to say, and the corpselike silence of the talib, the clothes are also a vow and help make of Baba a powerful symbol.[6]

The second category of references to "binding" in the lesson is "serial binding" or connecting through a series of links. There are three main series or chains recounted in the lesson. All connect back to Cenabi Hakk, the Sufi term for God.

Baba presented the first chain in episode 3 as the way I should begin my explanation of the murshid for my society. (It is noteworthy that when Baba presented the murshid for my personal understanding, he accomplished this through narrative and adage, without recourse to such a chain.) He began this third-party explanation with the statement that Cenabi Hakk could not always stay and guide humankind, so he sent the following people in his place:

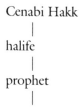

Cenabi Hakk
|
halife
|
prophet
|

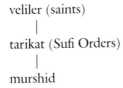

veliler (saints)
|
tarikat (Sufi Orders)
|
murshid

This is a quasi-historical chain in that the prophets are understood to have ended with the coming of Muhammad, and the tarikat or Sufi Orders to have appeared much later. But the top link of the chain, the halife, is also a clerical rank of the Bektashis. Baba explained that the role of the halife was to hold the place of God, while that of the prophet was to keep human beings from the prohibitions of God and work to make them truly human. As for the saints, some are hidden, some are known. The murshid then carries on with the guidance of individual talibs. I view this chain as a sort of logic, in that its function is to display connections and thereby to legitimize the place of the murshid cosmologically.

In the fifth episode, Baba brought up the two other chains of the lesson. These, too, function as cosmological binders. One is the chain of murshids of the founder of the Bektashi Order:

Cenabi Hakk
|
Lokman Perende
|
Ahmet Yesevî
|
Haji Bektash Veli

Lokman Perende and Ahmet Yesevî are two famous Sufi leaders from northeast Iran. Baba brought up this chain when we were discussing the difference between murshids whose spiritual guides are earthly (*pir-perver*) and those whose murshid is God (*Huda-perver*). Lokman Perende is part of this latter group.

In this same episode, Baba brought up yet a third chain in a discussion of supernatural powers of the saints. The power to perform miracles comes through this chain:

Cenabi Hakk
|

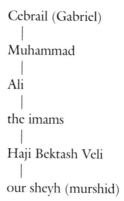

Cebrail (Gabriel)
|
Muhammad
|
Ali
|
the imams
|
Haji Bektash Veli
|
our sheyh (murshid)

Or, in a translation of Baba's words:

WE
.... with the esteemed Prophet~
.... we begin\
the Prophet and Gabriel
                              \from Gabriel upon whom be peace
Gabriel
       \upon whom be peace
from Cenabi Hakk he was brought~
thus~ we connect him
but after~
.. these~ to the esteemed Ali~
to the imams~
in turn until it comes to Haji Bektash~
from Haji Bektash in turn thus\
.. to our sheyh-
ah- they call this the "chain of the Order"

This chain is thus the chain of spiritual revelation and hence spiritual power. It differs from the chain described two episodes earlier (halife to murshid) in that it is more specific and, in mentioning Ali, emphasizes the Sufi or mystic revelation more. Baba's order of describing these two chains thus parallels again the outer to inward paradigm, from the more general Sufi to the more particularly Bektashi.

The importance to the Bektashis of the above chain is reflected in its having a specific name, *silsile-i tarikat,* and its being displayed in abbreviated form on a banner in the large public meeting room in the basement of the tekke. The banner hangs prominently between the Albanian and American flags, directly behind Baba's chair. On the banner are verses from the Qur'an, translated into Albanian and written in white letters. In the corners of the banner are the four names: Allah, Muhammad, Ali, Haji Bektash Veli. This replicates the silsile-i tarikat, the chain of spiritual knowledge. It also contrasts with a common Sunni pattern of putting the names of the first four caliphs—Abu Bakr, Omar, Othman, and Ali—in the four corners of pages of selected verses from the Qur'an. These four caliphs represent one form of succession after Muhammad. They were chosen by the Sunni community, but were not necessarily of the Prophet's bloodline, nor, apart from Ali, were they concerned with mystic understanding. The Bektashi banner is therefore an explicit keying and rejection of the Sunni pattern.

The third type of "binding" referred to in the lesson is what I termed "personal binding," or "binding with one in an immediate interaction." This definition is a hedge, though, for as I have described attunement, it certainly fits into personal binding. In fact, entering into a conversation implies at least a minimal sort of this binding. The whole lesson is clearly a kind of "personal binding." For the purposes of discussion here, however, I want to emphasize two special forms of this binding: explicit mention of Baba's and my relationship, and shared laughter.

Baba referred directly to our relationship in his affirmation of my narrative on coming to study with him:

> it is understood that Baba Bayram
> **assigned** {*havale etmek*} to me this "misfortune"

We both laughed after this, as we also laughed three episodes later when at the end of the seventh episode Baba voiced his confirmation:

> what can I do so~
> .. as for you~ you are **left over** from Baba Bayram

Baba Bayram was the initiating link through which I came to study with Baba. In this affirmation and confirmation Baba builds on and reinforces this link through explicit mention and through humor.

To review then, the sorts of references to binding and embodiments of it in the entire lesson are as follows:

episode 1   ritual binding
episode 2   shared laughter
episode 3   first chain
episode 4   naming and shared laughter
episode 5   second and third chains
episode 6   ritual binding and shared laughter
episode 7   naming and shared laughter
episode 8 to 11   ritual binding

These categorizations of binding are not independent, however, in that personal binding is transformed through ritual into cosmological binding. Ultimately, the purpose of all binding is the continuity of the chain of the Order.

Explicit concern for continuity through binding develops in the last episodes, in which Baba authorizes his friend Bayram (personal binding) to become a halife and baba (ritual binding), in hopes that the now "Baba" Bayram will take over the Michigan tekke (serial binding) when he, Baba Rexheb, dies. But this goal is thwarted when Baba Bayram dies in 1973. The attempt to secure the continuity of the tekke, referred to in the second episode when Baba and I were concerned about what would happen after Baba's death, is thus an underlying theme of the whole interaction. Baba's last words in the lesson are:

Baba: however HE {Baba Bayram}~
    ... while staying here~
                    {following in a faster, higher voice}
    I had always in mind that~
    . I don't want that~
{telephone rings}
    after me that the tekke~
    stay without a baba
FT: true-
Baba: without a leader\
    (so) I said~
    I am pleased~
    to write for you a letter~
    . and I will give it to Kâzim Baba~
    so that you~
    he confer being BOTH a baba on you~

                    and a halife\
                    what more\
FT: ahhhha
Baba: .... and GO there\
         he went\
         he said~
{telephone rings again}
FT: if you like Baba~
Baba: yaa
{noises and telephone rings yet again}

                    {end of lesson}

IV. Texture of Interaction with Baba

In the previous chapter I described the interaction of murshid and talib in terms of the keying "this is not a joust." I brought out how the talib, painfully aware of insecurities, is met not with confrontation but with skillful nurturing by the murshid. This leads to the talib's dependence on and trust in the murshid. The drama of the righting of my interaction with Baba, described earlier in terms of episodes and the pivot of the lesson, was thus a specific instance of the basic keying of the talib-murshid relationship.

In this chapter I continue to examine Baba's and my interaction in the Hizir lesson. Only whereas I earlier focused on structure, as in the structure of the episode and the lesson, here I consider cohesive interactions of a finer and more idiosyncratic nature. These interactions give the lesson a "texture" in the sense that they are patterns that occur throughout the text and that aesthetically hold the text together. Less dramatic than the bracketing of episodes or the designation of a pivot to the lesson, these more delicate games make up the distinctive pattern of Baba's teaching and my learning. They relate to questions of attention, to the reshaping of recollections, and to the drawing of connections across the text and between Baba and myself.

Readers unaccustomed to the scale of micro-analysis of conversation or those whose minds turn off at the sight of grammatical labeling may find themselves temporarily in a swamp here, their reading slowed. Do persevere; there is respite in the section on narrative retelling. In addition the different aesthetic that such close analysis implies requires at first exposure a patient eye.

Drawing on Each Other's Language

in which Baba and the student are shown to step to each other's languages, which verbal minuet occasionally takes off in a veritable Viennese waltz of attunement

During the course of the Hizir lesson, Baba and I draw on each other's languages in our talk. It is a common game we play[1] and clearly a form of attunement made more interesting thanks to the differences in our languages and the differences in the ways we shift back and forth. Such play toward the language of the other expresses both extent of previous interaction as well as the quality of current attention.

In the least restricted definition, "language of the other" is simply "a language that the other understands." Baba's translations of adages from Arabic or Persian into Turkish for me are obvious examples. The strangeness of the sounds of the "distant" language, along with its association with the Qur'an or Sufi poetry, catch my attention, whereupon Baba's translation brings the meaning home for me.

This interchange contributes yet another understanding of the murshid as intermediary. Earlier I noted how Baba had shown the murshid to be an "intercessor" between human beings and God. To this the epithet of "translator" should be added, for certainly the murshid translates from the Bektashi tradition to the understanding of the talib.

A second, more restricted way to define "language of the other" is as the "native language." In my case this is English, whereas in Baba's it is Albanian. We each share some fluency in the native language of the other, but our lessons have always been conducted in Turkish. Thus any use of our native languages is likely to stand out.[2]

In the Hizir lesson, Baba used English twice. The first time was in the first episode when he was introducing the essential point that, according to the Sufi Orders, there need to be intermediaries between humans and God. Baba started with the contrast of Sunni Islam:

Baba: . Sunnilikte~
     insan~ . Allah ile doğru **direct**~
     . alaka- alakali olmali\

     * * * * *

Baba: . in Sunnism~
     man~ . with God directly **direct**~
     . should be connec- connected\

In this remark, Baba first gave the Turkish *doğru,* which means "straight" or "direct," and then immediately translated into the English "direct." This use of my native language moved the dialogue into my verbal territory. It also embodied the idea of "directness," for to shift into another's language is iconic of directness.

The other time Baba used an English word in the Hizir lesson was also in the first episode, but during the important third incident of the Hizir narrative. Hizir, the murshid, is telling Musa, the would-be talib, how to act as they swam across the water.

```
Baba:  . benim yakami tut sen~
       . ve gel\
       swimming gibi
FT:                      haa {with breath, not voice}
Baba: gezeceklerdi\


       * * * * *

Baba:  . you hold onto my collar~
       . and come\
       . as if swimming
FT:                      haa {with breath, not voice}
Baba: they would cross over (travel)\
```

There is a playful quality to Baba's switch into English in the midst of his "sea of Turkish." Obviously from my remark, he caught my attention, although I would have understood the situation without the English.

As for my switching to Albanian, that did not occur in the Hizir lesson. But in a lesson several months earlier there is an interesting opening where Baba shifted, it appears absent-mindedly, into Albanian, and I then shifted into Albanian in my request to have him return to Turkish. (The Albanian is in bold.)

```
FT:   heyy Baba\
      nasılsınız bugün\
Baba: ehh .. iYIyim\
      mirë\
      jam mirë\
FT:                ehh
Baba:       shim do të themë apo~
FT:                            Ohh\
```

affedersiniz Baba\
në turkisht të lutem

* * * * *

FT: hey Baba\
how are you today\
Baba: ehh .. I'm FINE\
well
I'm well
FT: ehh
Baba: now **we will say or**~
FT: Ohh\
excuse me Baba\
in Turkish please

I see my use of Albanian here as different from the previous examples of Baba's uses of English, which stood out and drew attention by their strangeness. My use of Albanian does not stand out, but with a gentleness picks up on Baba's Albanian. It fosters a continuity, as if, despite the request for change, I do not want to jar Baba.

A third way to define "language of the other," in addition to "language that one understands" and "native language," is "dialect of the other." Baba and I speak different dialects of Turkish. He is the more fluent speaker, but his dialect is the more regionally marked one; my Turkish has non-native elements, but morphophonemically[3] is closer to the Standard Istanbul dialect.

Baba temporarily adopted features of my Turkish dialect—here distinctive non-native usages—in several places in the Hizir lesson, notably in the second episode. This was the episode described in detail in chapter two. The example occurred when Baba was developing the adage "nothing is ever lost" (hiç bir şey gayip **olmaz**). I repeated his point, but in repeating changed the verbal auxiliary (*olmak*) to one less appropriate to the situation (*etmek*). Baba picked up on my nonstandard usage for a while.

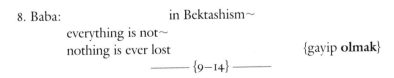

8. Baba: in Bektashism~
everything is not~
nothing is ever lost   {gayip **olmak**}
——— {9–14} ———

15. FT: . but- no- that is . important things are not lost
           [it means-   {gayip **etmek**}
16. Baba: not lost   {gayip **etmek**}
          yeah\
          .. everything- uhh and there is a philosopher\
17. FT: yes\
18. Baba:
          eh who says that~
                  nothing is ever lost   {gayip **etmek**}
          I don't know which philosopher
19. FT: [yes
20. Baba: [who said this\
          that nothing is ever lost   {gayip **olmak**}

In the end (turn 20), Baba went back to the auxiliary (*olmak*) that he began with and that he normally uses in that phrase. Baba's temporary movement into my dialect did not draw my attention. It simply built unobtrusively on my earlier turn. If anything, it attested to Baba's attention to my language. Indeed, this is the pattern whenever Baba moves into my dialect: he picks up on my language of a preceding turn.

In contrast, when I move into Baba's dialect of Turkish, which I do frequently in the fourth episode of the Hizir lesson, it is not as a reflection of Baba's language in closely preceding turn. The fourth episode was the one in which I naively began by asking Baba for more stories. There followed several passages of remedy and mediation before this error was righted. At the start of the first remedy, when I had just realized something was wrong, I began with a phrase using a locative postposition when ordinarily I would use a dative. (In other parts of the lesson, with the same verb *koymak*, I use the more standard dative.) Such use of a locative when Standard Turkish calls for a dative is characteristic of Baba's Rumelian dialect (Kowalski, 1933).

FT: .. heyy Baba\
    ben . şey .
    tape'**de**   koydum   bunu\
    {tape + loc.   I-put   this + accus}
    eve giderim

* * * * *

FT: .. heyy Baba\
   I . say .
   I put this **on** the tape\
   I'll go home

In the fourth episode, and especially in my narrative of how I came to study with Baba, there are other, similar examples of my temporarily adopting features of Baba's West Rumelian dialect (Nemeth, 1956, 1961; Friedman, 1982). (More conveniently, see Appendix C.) Such examples from my narrative there include fossilized suffixes (*şansli, yoldaydi, bulayim, kuzhinade*), as well as locatives when normally I would use datives (*baktım telefon kitabında, geldik yeni salonda, geldim üçüncü kere kuzhinade*).

Another instance in which I shifted into Baba's dialect during the Hizir lesson was at the very outset of taping, when I asked Baba the date in order to index the tape and check whether the machine was picking up both our voices. There I began in Turkish, asking if today was November fifteen, then immediately changed into Baba's more common form, asking if it was the fifteen*th* of November. As in other examples of my use of Baba's dialect forms, this usage did not mirror immediately preceding discourse. My movement into Baba's distinctive dialect, at the level of morphophonemics and morphology, is instead a sort of anticipatory accommodation (Giles et al., 1973; Trudgill, 1986). In contrast, all of Baba's accommodations to my peculiar dialect in Turkish immediately follow my use of its distinctive structures. That is, Baba's accommodation is responsive whereas mine is anticipatory.

Baba's movement into my dialect of Turkish builds on my preceding language and, as such, establishes a continuity. It does not draw attention during the exchange, but interestingly enough, neither do my "unprecedented" movements into Baba's dialect of Turkish draw attention. Perhaps these features are below our level of consciousness during the interaction. Whatever the case, additional insight into our drawing on each other's dialect can be gleaned from noting where in the interaction such moves take place.

My movement into Baba's dialect of Turkish occurred in places of anxiety—at the start of taping, when trying repeatedly to negotiate discussion, when initiating a remedy, and when elaborating a mediation. All these are moments when deference is appropriate. Given that my dialect of Turkish is generally closer to the Istanbul dialect than Baba's, and therefore considered "better Turkish," it is not surprising that I do not wish to lord this over Baba at such times. Again though, this is an explanation born from analysis; during the encounter I do not think either of us consciously noticed such shifts.

In contrast, Baba shifted into my dialect of Turkish not at moments of anxiety for him but rather at times in which he was developing a point. This pattern of building on my language is most dramatic in Baba's movement into my syntax. Here is yet a fourth way to describe "language of the other." Besides "language that one understands," "native language," or "particular dialect," "language of the other" can also be construed as "immediately preceding syntactic constructions." Such movement by Baba is common in the early parts of episodes when a sort of entree to discussion is being negotiated. This was especially true of the opening section of the whole Hizir lesson.

There, in my second attempt to negotiate entree to discussion, I made the point that I did not see relationships like that of murshid and talib in America today. Baba responded that there were no murshids here. He did this in such a way that his substitution of "murshid" for my "relationship of murshid and talib" was highlighted.

25. FT: .... I do not see now in America\
                                 \ such a close relationship
                                 \ of talib and murshid

          [zaten
26. Baba: **[za-**
27. FT: **burda yok**
28. Baba: **zaten murşid yok burda**
29. FT: eh\
30. Baba: murşid da yok burda\

I left the second part in Turkish to highlight the closeness of our utterances. Notice first in the preceding line how Baba and I start to say the same word (*zaten*, "certainly") simultaneously (turns 25 and 26). But then notice how Baba's ensuing construction parallels mine.

25 and 27. FT: zaten   burda   yok
              (certainly) (here)   (it is not)
                                   (the close relationship of
                                   murshid and talib)

28. Baba: zaten   murşid   yok   burda
              (certainly) (murshid) (it is not) (here)

It is important to know that in Turkish, whose word order is much more flexible than that of English, the place of primary emphasis is just before the verb. In Baba's response, he inserted the word "murshid" in the place of emphasis, relegating the adverb (*burda*) to the end. This change was a substitution not of the adverb, but rather of my whole preceding phrase "such a close relationship of talib and murshid" (turn 25). Baba's point was that there were not even murshids here, let alone murshid-talib relations. To emphasize his point yet further, Baba then added:

30. Baba: murSID   da   yok   burda
       (a MURshid)   (even)   (it is not)   (here)

Here he stressed the word "murshid" and added *da,* meaning "even" or "too," in the place of emphasis before the verb. Baba then declared how professors were not murshids. Like earlier sorts of attunement to my language, this reflection of my syntactic structure maintained a continuity in which the one change then stood out. As for my participation in this game, in my isolated responses I do not find such close reflecting of Baba's immediately preceding syntax

However I do find precise reflection of both of each other's syntax in certain remarkable passages in the Hizir lesson. These passages provide yet another way of understanding the "language of the other." And whereas the fourth way of understanding "language of the other" was as "immediately preceding syntactic constructions," this fifth and final way of understanding "language of the other" is as the "immediately preceding phrases," including thereby both syntax and morphology.

This reciprocal reflecting of the other's language is a sort of extended "tracking," or picking up on a phrase of the previous speaker's utterance. Such tracking is often accompanied with "latching," or timing of change of turns so closely that there is not a perceivable pause between them.

The first example of such a passage is a familiar one from chapter two. It took place near the end of the second episode.

41. FT: ellerden\
     ellere~
     ellerden\
42. Baba: **ellere**~
     gayip **olmadi**\

43. FT: olmadı\
44. Baba: **şimdiye kadar**\
45. FT: **şimdiye kadar**\
46. Baba: yaa\
47. FT: ama **bugünler** Baba~
48. Baba: **bugünler**~
         . bakalım\   {all in softer voice}
         ne olur\

         * * * * *

41. FT: from hands\
          to hands~
          from hands\
42. Baba: **to hands**~
          it was **not lost**\
43. FT: **not lost**\
44. Baba: **up to now**\
45. FT: **up to now**\
46. Baba: yaa\
47. FT: but **in these days** Baba?
48. Baba: **in these days**~
          .let us see\   {all in softer voice}
          what will be\

The first example of tracking (turn 42, *ellere*) is also an example of Baba picking up on a nonstandard form from my immediately preceding turn. (My use of a plural in turn 41, *-ler*, marks the phrase as non-native; the more common form in this phrase would be a singular.) Notice too how Baba has not just picked up on the phrase "to hands," but on the progression "from hands to hands."

In my next turn I tracked Baba's auxiliary *olmadi*. In my subsequent turn, I tracked Baba's "until today," after which Baba tracked my phrase "these days." The back-and-forth of our timing is as tightly coordinated as are our words. It is so close that I wonder if we are hearing each other or rather predicting closely. If the latter, then this prediction is not just of words but of syntax and semantics as well.

It would be difficult to separate careful repetition from close prediction. But the second example of tracking, in which I pick up Baba's auxiliary "olmadi," provides an interesting if inconclusive perspective. Earlier in the episode, I had used a different auxiliary ("etmek" instead of "olmak") with the same phrase. Here, though, I pick up Baba's auxiliary, but I do it within my morphophonemic system. Baba's "olmadi," with its lack of vowel harmony, reflects his West Rumelian dialect (Nemeth, 1956), but I maintain my own more Standard Turkish form of "olmadı" with vowel harmony. This example might lend support to the notion that such tracking is not blind repetition. The question is, Do I hear Baba's distinctive form and do I have both possible forms in my system? Rather than getting mired in this, I suggest that I probably hear the beginning of Baba's word and predict on that basis, but in my own morphophonemics. So his final syllable would be irrelevant.

In either case, the more interesting question is, How do two people of radically different lingual backgrounds arrive at the point of being able to coordinate so deftly or predict so swiftly? I propose that this comes from countless previous interactions, previous playful recollections of dialogue with the other. And I think that it is no accident that this play surfaces at a time of coming together over the vital concern of how to face the uncertain future of the tekke when Baba is dead.

To mark such a passage, I call it an "attunement slide." With this special name I want to emphasize the clarity of expression of attunement in drawing on each other's language and the probable density of previous attunements that facilitate it. I discussed another example of attunement slide at the end of the Introduction, when in the dialogue I was checking what Baba had meant by miracles of the murshids. (The passage included reference to the story of Haji Bektash Veli riding on a stone.)

In addition to that attunement slide, there is yet a third instance of attunement slide in the Hizir lesson. This example includes not only tracking, but a variety of ways in which Baba and I draw on each other's languages. It is therefore a fitting example with which to close this section.

The passage is part of my third attempt to negotiate discussion on the murshid and talib in the first episode of the Hizir lesson. I began this effort by reframing the matter of the murshid and talib in terms of my Christian religious tradition. This attempt was finally successful. In particular, notice below the multiple strategies of drawing on each other's languages (these are in boldface and named to the right), before Baba reframed in terms of Sunni Islam.

43. FT: ... but also Baba~
           in the Christian {"**Hıristiyan**"} journey~   {translation}
           . er- heritage~
44. Baba: ya

45. FT: I do not see murshids\
     Jesus~ {"hazreti Isa"}   {translation}
     was a murshid\
46. Baba: yes\
47. FT: this is clear\
48. Baba: **the "havariyun" too were murshids**\   {syntax}
49. FT: who baba?
50. Baba: 'havariyun'
          .. **apostol**\   {back *o* as in "open"}   {translation}
51. FT: . **apostol**\   {more centralized *o* as in "hot"} {tracking}
52. Baba: they were **murshid**
53. FT: **murshid**   {tracking}
54. Baba: they were\
          because they made clear
          Christianity\ ("**Kristiyanlıki**")   {translation}
55. FT: true\
          but from them\ **after?**
56.   **after**~   {tracking}
          . there were none\
          how~
          because
          . as in Sunnism~

The three sorts of drawing on each other's languages illustrated in this passage are: translation, syntactic mirroring, and tracking. Of these, only the translation aspect differs somewhat from examples given earlier in this section.

Unlike Baba's translations from distant texts into Turkish, or either of our use of the other's native language, my translation here is of Christian religious names into Islamic forms. That is, although my comments refer to Christianity (my native religious background), by choosing certain forms, I "translate" them to Baba's native religious frame of Islam.

The clearest example of this translation is in turn 45, where my term for Jesus (*Isa*) and especially the title (*hazreti*) are distinctly Muslim. Jesus is accorded the stature of a prophet by Islam, which is obviously different from Christians' understanding. My reference with Muslim names moves Jesus from a Christian into a Muslim frame. Similarly, but in a different direction, Baba's translation of *havariyun* to *apostol* moves toward my language and religious frame. In fact there is an almost tennis volley quality, of each giving to the other's frame, to our attunement here, as I move toward Islam and Baba toward Christianity. This movement toward each other's frame is clearest in our ways of referring to "Christian." I use the Turkish and common Muslim form—*Hıristiyan* (turn 43), while Baba uses *Kristiyan* (turn 54)—a more Western or Christian-sounding form.

Also in this passage, Baba attunes to my syntactic construction:

45. FT: hazreti Isa   mursid   idi\
           (his majesty Jesus) (a murshid)   (was)

To which Baba responds:

48. Baba: havariyun da   murshid   idiler\
          (the apostles too)   (murshids)   (were)\

Baba maintains my syntax, but in substituting "the apostles too" for my initial phrase "his majesty Jesus," he continues the series from Jesus to the apostles.

Baba then translates "havariyun" to "apostol," which I track, but in a form closer to my English pronunciation. More tracking and latching (turns 52 to 56) follow on both our parts. It is as if this interchange is a warmup, after which Baba signals entree to discussion. He draws the parallel of Christianity with Sunni Islam and then contrasts Sunni Islam, and its lack of intermediaries, with Sufi Islam and the important presence of its intermediaries. This passage, with its multiple instances of closely packed attunement, clearly illustrates again the contagious nature of strategies of attunement. And it leads into Baba's central point of the murshid being an intermediary.

The other attunement slide described in this section ("from hands to hands") also led into a critical issue—how Baba faced not knowing how the tekke would continue after his death. The coordination and joint attention to each other's language to which these attunement slides attest are fitting settings of important messages.

The Resonance of Retelling

in which Baba's retelling of the story of Hizir and Musa sets up most potent learning for the student: in the current episode, in revising understanding of an earlier narrative, and later with a future narrative of the lesson

Important messages by Baba are often preceded by attunement slides—those passages of dense tracking and latching where Baba and I build on each other's immediately preceding talk as well as on memories of earlier such shared talk. If we look beyond the buildup of important messages to the messages themselves, we find that these are often framed as retellings of special narratives. Such retellings are especially effective in securing and reshaping my understanding of relationships.

A prime example of the shaping and reshaping of recollections to convey a message occurs in the first episode of the Hizir lesson. There Baba's critical message was that in Sufi Islam, unlike Sunni Islam, there are intermediaries between human beings and God. The murshid is that intermediary. The buildup to this message was first an attunement slide (described at the end of the previous section), followed by a quick likening of Christianity with Sunni Islam, and an equally swift contrasting of these forms with Sufi Islam. At that point Baba recited again a short adage that he had recited at the outset of the episode, and then delivered his message of the murshid being an intermediary.

This message was then illustrated and reinforced by Baba's recounting of two narratives: one long narrative that he told immediately and another shorter narrative that he recounted thirty minutes later in the lesson. The long narrative resonated with previous tellings of a similar story, and also with a different, earlier narrative whose understanding had to be recast in light of the long narrative. The new understanding that emerged reinforced Baba's message in the Hizir lesson that the murshid is an intermediary, and more specifically an intercessor.

Like the adage that preceded Baba's message, this first, long narrative was particularly memorable because it was a retelling. Just as Baba had played into the syntax of my preceding clauses (as described in the last section), so in the retelling, Baba played into the "syntax" of incidents of my memory of the story as he had told it to me before.

The particular narrative was the one of Hizir, the murshid, and his would-be talib, Musa. Baba had told me this story several times before the Hizir lesson. I cannot anchor the first telling with a date, but I have a version of it on tape from five months before the November lesson. This experience of previous tellings heightened the predictability of the telling during the Hizir lesson. As evidence of this greater predictability, my few comments during the telling (supplying two words and a phrase that Baba sought) showed I was following closely and predicting accurately. One result of such heightened predictability is that both speaker and listener are freed for more subtle forms of communication, including attention to any changes in the retelling.

The main differences in the retelling during the Hizir lesson were the frame and point of the whole story. In earlier tellings, the frame had generally been my impatience, for, like Musa, I have trouble waiting. Here though, Baba expressly set the story as an illustration of the message that the murshid is centrally an intermediary.

This is the dialogue that just precedes his narrative:

Baba: for he is very much an intermediary\
　　　　　　　　　　　　　　　　\the murshid\
FT:　　yes
Baba: and even~
　　　　there are also many stories about these
FT:　　　　　　　　　　　　　　　　　hmm
Baba: that is in the time of Hazreti Musa

Baba then moved directly into the story.

The story is an old one; a version of it is found in the Qur'an in the Sura of the Cave.[4] As outlined in chapter two, in the discussion of the narrative pattern of the "word and its vindication," Musa came to Hizir, wanting to be his talib, but Hizir was not encouraging. He told Musa that Musa would not make it, that he would not be able to be patient with him. Musa remonstrated, and then Hizir finally agreed, on the condition that Musa never question his actions.

In Baba's previous tellings of the story there followed two incidents (similar to the first and third incidents in the Qur'anic version) in which Musa could not restrain himself from questioning Hizir's seemingly callous actions. Hizir then announced that that was enough and Musa clearly could not stay with him, but before leaving he would explain what had been outwardly bizarre actions. The story closed with the lines from the Qur'anic version of the story in which Hizir reiterated his initial point that Musa could not endure and be patient with him.

The major change in Baba's November telling was the addition of a third incident, which was utterly unlike any in the Qur'anic version of the story. It was much more a Sufi episode, whose point was that the murshid is the way through which the student reaches God. Thus Baba's telling me the story over several months as well as this telling with its third incident are progressions from a more limited orthodox understanding to the deeper Sufi understanding.

One explanation of the difference in Baba's tellings could be that in earlier situations Baba's point had been my lack of patience. Two of the Qur'anic incidents were sufficient to foreground this. In contrast, in this lesson Baba's point had been the crucial role of the murshid, for which a decidedly Sufi incident was needed. But another interpretation of the gradual revealing of the third incident was that I had progressed and was at the point where Baba could share more of the Sufi way with me. From this point of view the earlier omission of the third incident had been a form of silence.

Silence is most important to the Sufis. Among its many uses, it is considered the appropriate response to those who are not ready for certain spiritual knowledge. So in telling me the third incident, Baba not only shared the Sufi insight of the incident, he also made me more aware of silence as a feature of learning in our relationship.

This third incident, which was referred to in the discussion of ritual binding (chapter three), was where Hizir commanded Musa to swim across the water with him, holding onto his collar, and all the time saying "Pir Hakk," "The Pir [patron saint, here murshid] is the Truth." Musa, however, showed his lack of trust in Hizir by reconsidering halfway across the water and calling out to God instead, at which point he began to drown. In his explanation, Baba made clear that it was Hizir's place to call out to Cenabi Hakk (Sufi term for God) for both of them; as for Musa, his place was to call out only to Hizir. If both called out to God, then that would signify separation between them, and to whom should God respond?

By sharing this incident with me, Baba not only expanded my understanding, but also bestowed trust. No talk of trust was necessary though, for the attunement of previous shared tellings brought with it collusion. One change—in this case the addition of an incident within the old framework—and focus on the murshid as intermediary was achieved, and Baba's and my relationship was strengthened with added trust and shared experience. This is a clear example of reinforcement of a message through the retelling of a narrative, but still it does not show the full power of a retelling to reinforce a message. Baba's retelling, and thereby his message, was especially memorable in the Hizir lesson because the retelling also resonated with a different narrative that Baba had told me four months earlier. It forced me to recast my understanding of a significant part of that narrative.

The earlier narrative was on the life of Ali Baba (1826–1905), the murshid of Baba's murshid. In that story Ali, who was still a dervish, was serving his murshid at Bektashi headquarters in central Anatolia, when his murshid ordered him back to Albania to oversee a difficult tekke there. Ali Baba tried to refuse this assignment by arguing that he did not want to leave the side of his murshid, and furthermore he had heard that the people of that place in Albania (Baba's home town) were a cantankerous lot. His murshid countered and closed the matter by stating the following.

> as for YOU . wherever you are~
> .... I I-I- there will I be\
> with him- together I will be with you\
> .. on that account do not worry\

{sound of prayer beads through hand of Baba}

> .... and~
> .... coming to your second question~
> ...... you

{sound of prayer beads through hand of Baba}

> ...... open your mouth
> .. and I~ ..... **I will speak for you**\

(The line in boldface is the one on which I will focus.)

Ali Baba then went to the tekke in Albania, where he soon found himself in a life-threatening situation. At that moment, back in central Turkey, his murshid became aware of the danger. He had been drinking coffee with the other babas there when he suddenly paused with his cup held in the air, halfway to his lips. Then he put the cup down and remarked to the other babas that Ali Baba had been in danger but that Cenabi Hakk had saved him. During this time back in Albania, however, there had been no grand scene or dialogue.

My point is that I had thought that when the murshid promised to "speak for Ali Baba," he meant he would put words in his mouth when speaking to other men. But Baba's subsequent telling of the story of Hizir and Musa, specifically his explanation of the third incident, told me that for a murshid to "speak for someone" (for Hizir to speak for Musa) implied "speaking to God for one," in other words, intercession.

Baba's telling of the Hizir and Musa story reinforced his message of the murshid as intermediary through contrast with previous tellings and previous messages of these tellings. The retelling itself in the Hizir lesson was made more memorable in that it evoked a recasting of understanding of yet another earlier story.

There is still a third way in which Baba's telling of the story of Hizir and Musa helped reinforce his message of the murshid as intermediary. In this I look ahead in the Hizir lesson rather than back to narratives from previous lessons. In particular I consider the sixth episode of the Hizir lesson. It was there that I had asked Baba why it was that we knew of great teachers through the writings of their students. Baba had immediately replied that this was *üfürüş* or "inspiration." He had then told the short story about the Baba who was asked why he had not written anything. The baba answered that he was not given anything to write. As Baba expanded, all that one "sees" or "writes" in spiritual matters is "in-come" from God through one's murshid. He especially cited nefes as such "in-come" from the murshid. In other words, there, too, the murshid is the intermediary.

In making this point, Baba was referring back to his telling of the story of Hizir and Musa thirty minutes earlier, whose point was to show the murshid as intermediary. The later discussion, by referring back to the same word, *vasita* (intermediary), of the earlier discussion expanded my understanding of "intermediary." Before, I had understood it as the means to reach God, but now with the added example of "inspiration," I could see that it meant to receive from God as well.

In terms of attention then, Baba's retellings of narratives heighten rather than lessen attention. When a story is retold, attention can be given to subtler differences in the new telling or to resonances with the listener's everchanging storehouse of memories. In terms of texture, retellings add a whole dimension to a text. But, as I have tried to show in this section, the meaning of this added dimension can also be related to the texture of the relationship of the teller and listener—here, to the trust between Baba and myself.

The Learning of "Sophistry" and the Pleasure in "Misfortune"

> in which the learning of "sophistry" is a joyful gift, the pleasure in "misfortune" a strengthening of bonds, and the nefes reemerges as a prototype of drawing connections

A possible overview of the way Baba teaches, as shown so far in this chapter, is that Baba first encourages a continuity—of dialect, syntax, or narrative telling—and then shapes his point in contrast to that continuity. Although this delineation of teaching into a two-step process clarifies in one sense, it is ultimately misleading. Baba's actions are more unified. Additionally misleading in such a construction is the sense of Baba as agent and the talib as present but passive. In fact, learning with Baba is active on the part of the talib as well. A better summary of the way Baba teaches,[5] and one that does not ride roughshod over the texture and pleasure of the process, would be to say that Baba constantly draws playful connections in our talk, so much so that I cannot but join in.

Indeed, in the last section I focused on connections that *I* had drawn: from Baba's retelling of the Hizir narrative to previous tellings of that story, and from Baba's retelling to a different, earlier narrative. Baba's message, that the murshid is the intermediary between human beings and God, was memorably forged through these connections. I concluded with a connection that I felt *Baba* drew through use of the word *vasita* (intermediary) in the first episode and then again in the sixth episode. The message of this connection was both a unifying of the lesson and an expanded understanding of the murshid, from murshid as intercessor to murshid as agent of poetic inspiration.

Now I present two more examples of Baba drawing connections across the Hizir lesson. I devote a whole section to these instances because I see this playful drawing of connections—this attunement—as our essential action.

The first instance involves a single word. It stands out in the lesson because it is a word I did not know before the lesson. By the end of the lesson, however, I was able to appreciate a joke that hinges on that word. The word is *safsata,* or "sophistry." It first came up twenty-five minutes into the lesson, near the end of the fourth episode, the episode of repeated mediation. There, I had been making the point, as a compliment to Baba, that my society could stand to learn something from the Bektashis.

FT: for America\
    that~
    .. wha- what does Bektashism have to say
    -to this?
Baba: good
FT: maybe the universities TOO
    will learn a little\
    beca-
Baba: of course\

FT: this
Baba: they will take note that~
      what is this\
FT: . so much-
Baba: "**safsata**" is this\
FT: pardon~ {"my sir"}
Baba: "safsata"
      is this\
      what it is\
              "safsata" do you know?
      that is~
      un- is this something without import~
      that's what they call sophistry in Arabic\
FT: . ahh there are some professors BaBA
      who wouldn't say as much\
      .. who would be interested there Baba\
Baba: ya\
FT: eh those-
      with them I will work\
      as for the others hey
Baba: go-
FT: to the sea with them\
      may they amuse themselves there but~
Baba and FT: {laughter}

It was after this interchange that I proclaimed my second aphoristic
affirmation to the effect that true teachers must be murshids. Baba agreed,
but with the qualification that I must mean "perfected" murshids. Then
he recited couplets from a nefes by Niyazi. Within these couplets Baba
brought up safsata again, this time as a modification of the second line of
the nefes. This line usually reads:

    yolunu sarpa uğradır   his way will lead to difficulty

Baba modified this line, however, to include the recently evoked "safsata":

    yalnız saf(sa)ta öğretir   he teaches only false ways

Notice how Baba maintained the rhythm and rhyme scheme in the
above poetic line, despite his modification. This ability is highly valued

among Albanian Bektashis. (Indeed I have witnessed public arguments wherein messages for tombstones were criticized on the basis of the rhythm of the phrasing.)

Baba had first brought up the word "safsata," but when he had noted my incomprehension, he immediately gave an explanation of the word, and soon thereafter worked it into a nefes. Then, twenty minutes later, in the sixth episode when we were discussing inspiration in poetry, Baba made the point about inspiration being "in-come" from one's murshid. To elaborate this he explained that it came "from the heart"—which is the seat of higher faculties of perception—and that it was brought to the heart by Cenabi Hakk or one's murshid as intermediary. As reinforcement of this point, Baba brought up the example of sentimental poetry (as opposed to spiritual poetry), wherein if the poet has not himself experienced the feelings he writes of, he writes only safsata.

```
Baba: but how is it brought to the heart~
       who brings it to the heart~
                                    {in much lower voice}
       Cenabi Hakk
FT:                                  {also in low voice}
                    ohh-ohh
Baba:                  or one's murshid\
FT:                                    yes\
Baba: he brings it too so that
       HA\
       "say this"\
FT:            yes\
Baba:             "say this"~
       at that time he says that\
       that is HE is the intermediary\
FT:                              hmmmm
Baba: . if not~
       true poetry~ is THAT\
FT:                      yes
Baba: ... for example~
       ah- . poetry
              \ . that "poetry of feeling" {as opposed to the spiritual
                                           poetry that is nefes}
       If HE (the poet) is without any feeling~
       . he cannot write anything~
```

FT: true
Baba: because if he writes that-
     that- that is **sophistry** {safsata}\
FT: {chuckle}
Baba: {joins in chuckle}

Playfully and artfully, with humor and verse, Baba had set the scene for my learning. "Sophistry" was now mine for good.

The other example of Baba drawing connections across the Hizir lesson is his confirmation in the closing of episode 7 that links back with his affirmation to my narrative in episode 4. These connect through their humor and their common reference to me and Baba Bayram.

In episode 4 I told the story of how I came to study with Baba as a way of mediating Baba's comment that he wished that I rise high, which itself was mediation for my remedy of asking for other stories. Early in the narrative Baba thanked me, for he grasped the point of the narrative. But once I had begun, I kept on until I got to the point where Baba Bayram suggested I study with Baba:

FT: but then I came a second time~
     and a third time I think~
     when in the kitchen~
     Baba Bayram said~
          why don't you come
          and take lessons with Baba
     do you remember this?
Baba: ya
FT: Baba Bayram said that
     you should take lessons
     with Baba Rexheb
Baba: that means~
     so it's to be understood that **it was Baba Bayram
     who assigned to me this misfortune**\
FT and Baba: {shared laughter}

After our laughter, I repeated how fortunate I was, Baba thanked me again, and then he mediated my story by saying what pleasure it gave him that I wanted to understand what was the Truth. To this I noted that I had now been coming to the tekke for so many years, with my son, too, and that now it was as our home. Baba responded that, of course, I was his daughter, his child, as all children are one to Bektashi babas.

Twenty-six minutes later, after my misery with being unable to follow Baba's description of how the nefes by Nesimi had itself been written in circles, Baba again mediated my loss of face. I accepted his mediation, including his comment that I had learned much from him, and then thanked him for the lesson.

```
Baba:       as for you you listen\
        it stays in your memory~
        then what~
                    if there are books too~              {in lower pitch}
                    you look in the book how~ (it goes)
        thus it is\
FT:                         ehhh {accord}
        ... thus it is good Baba\
        .. ehh
        . eyyyy
        .. ey what a good lesson you have given
        today [Baba
Baba:       [eh well what can I do so
        .. as for you~ you are left over from Baba Bayram\
FT and Baba:                        {joint laughter}
```

The humor in this and Baba's above affirmation is welcome relief to the seriousness of the mediations of both preceding passages. I mentioned earlier the ritual dimensions of having been invited to study with Baba by another baba, but here I would emphasize the warmth of the association. Baba Bayram was Baba's best friend both in Egypt and in his years in America. To be linked with him—either assigned as a "misfortune," or "left over" from him—is no small thing.

The latter confirmation also provides a reading for the whole preceding lesson. That is, what can Baba do but humor me and my questions, as I am left over from his friend. In addition, this confirmation in the seventh episode connects to the affirmation of the fourth episode, both of which connect to Baba's and my initial coming together for study through the suggestion of Baba Bayram twelve years before. Thus, through connections across the lesson, Baba's and my connection has been celebrated. Further, in so linking the interaction and the interactants, Baba has brought closure. Mikhail Bakhtin[6] has proposed that one of the goals of works of art is to offer closure; Baba's attunements as described here are of that class.

As noted earlier, Baba is not the only one to draw connections; his very skill and humor in relating words, narratives, and incidents is contagious. For example, at the end of an earlier lesson about the life of Ali Baba, who was Baba's murshid's murshid, Baba initiated closure with the poem that Ali Baba had composed and dictated to his talib in his last hours. I asked Baba for a translation of the poem because it was in Persian. Baba translated it into Turkish. Then I thanked Baba for the lesson, but at the end of the thanking asked whether Ali Baba had been the one with the long eyebrows. This was a powerful connection of Ali Baba with Baba, for as Baba then happily brought up,

Baba: OO ah ah evet\
    ona~ çunkı~
    . ben hatırıma gelmiyor bu- derdi
    ukh- bir der- dervişin biri derdi bana ki~
        oouu sen Ali Babaya benzersin~
        bu uzun kaşlari boyle\

     * * * * *

Baba: OO ah ah yes\
    to him~ because~
    . I it didn't come to mind this one- said
    ukh- a der- one of the dervishes said to me that~
        oouu you look like Ali Baba
        with those long eyebrows\

As the entire lesson had been on the life of Ali Baba, my remembering this vignette that Baba must have told me at an earlier date, and then bringing it up at the end of a lesson on Ali Baba, were also linkings of interaction with interactant. Again, as with Baba's linking around the pivot of the Hizir lesson, the linking of interaction with interactants provides powerful closure.

This sort of closure-inducing linkage has been formalized in nefes, in which the last quatrain always has the pen name of the poet worked into the verse. In addition, there is always another sort of linkage in the reciting of nefes, and this often unexpressed linkage is between the reciter of the nefes and the person from whom he or she learned the nefes. This is a critical linkage, for at some level all re-citings of nefes are celebrations of that context of learning, of that sharing.

In the Hizir lesson, during the pivotal episode, Baba recited the quatrain on music and poetry and then made explicit the often unexpressed linkage:

Baba: .. eh Selim Baba soylemiş buni\
        .. Nesimiden gormıs, o
FT: evet\
Baba: .. Nesiminin divanında~

        * * * * *

Baba: .. eh Selim Baba had said this\
        .. he had "seen" it from Nesimi
FT: yes\
Baba: from the divan of Nesimi~

Nesimi is a famous fourteenth-century Sufi poet, but the important point is Baba's remark that he had learned the quatrain from Selim Baba, that is, from his own murshid. In general I would expect the murshid to be the source of many nefes that a talib learns; certainly that is true in my case. This, then, is a fourth understanding of the murshid as intermediary.

As Baba made clear in the third incident of the narrative on Hizir and Musa, the murshid is the intercessor between talib and God; and as he added in the sixth episode of that lesson, the murshid is also the agent of poetic inspiration. Then, as I pointed out in this chapter, the murshid is the translator to the language of the talib, and finally, he is also the main source of nefes, the spiritual songs.

Altogether the various aspects of the murshid's role suggest an understanding of nefes as playgrounds of connecting motifs. For I now understand the Hizir lesson as a sort of "prose nefes" whose main texture and action is the playful drawing of connections by and between Baba and myself. The full definition of a lesson, however, is the substance of the next chapter.

V. Bektashi Frame of Learning

In this study of an ongoing relationship with a Bektashi murshid, I have focused on episodic attunement over the course of a seventy-minute lesson, on the keying of Baba and myself in this lesson, and on finer and more far-reaching attunement in and beyond the lesson. I have not yet discussed the lesson itself as a meaningful entity. Rather, with a structuralist slight of hand, I defined the lesson in terms of its parts. I looked at internal brackets of the lesson, but did not consider the external brackets.

In this chapter I propose a framing of the lesson based on a Bektashi keying. This approach is similar to that of the third chapter, in which I described a keying of interaction between murshid and talib. In other words, unlike chapters two and four, in which I sought histories of attunement across the lesson, here I explore how the lesson relates to other activities at the tekke.

In Search of a Frame for the Lesson

> in which the fuzziness of the edges of the lesson are decried, and the central keying of nefes resorted to

My earlier focus on internal brackets to the exclusion of external ones was a conscious decision. The internal brackets were negotiated boundaries and, as I was interested in Baba's and my interaction, these were important loci of information. As for external brackets, they, too, would be important sources of information. Like a frame, they would cue expectation and interpretation of the interaction. But the reason I did not consider these external brackets earlier was that I had difficulty defining them.

In a gross spatial way, my arrival at the tekke and later departure from the tekke could be considered external brackets of the lesson. However, these moments enclose all manner of activity besides the lesson, including eating lunch and then visiting Baba's sister in an apartment adjoining the Tekke.

Another possible frame is greeting and leave-taking of Baba. Both greeting and leave-taking are performed with the ritual actions of bending down, taking Baba's hand, kissing it, and placing it to my forehead. But within these actions, besides the lesson, there is also the time of lunch and talking with the other people who live at the tekke.

The sharing of food or drink provides a third possible external bracketing of the lesson. Coffee is brought up to us in the study room near the start of the lesson, and lunch often determines the close of the lesson. When the coffee is brought up, however, we may still be talking of general matters, or I may be answering letters for Baba. The coffee is a more coincidental event, and lunch an interruptive one.

My unsuccessful efforts to determine external brackets lead me to the conclusion that for the lesson alone I do not find ritualized brackets that set it off from other activities. The lesson often begins with an awkward pause on my part. It closes with acknowledgment of outside demands such as a ringing telephone or a call to lunch. All this suggests that another approach is called for. Instead of looking for external brackets, which presuppose some entity that I call "the lesson," I turn instead to a keying of the lesson in Bektashi terms to provide a framework for interpretation.

Keying is the systematic signaling of how an activity is to be interpreted in terms of another known frame. In the third chapter I proposed the negatively defined keying of the interaction of murshid and talib as "this is not a joust." Here, in the fifth chapter, I seek a positively defined keying of the lesson in Bektashi terms.

The characteristic Bektashi form that signals a keying of the lesson is nefes. In the lessons, nefes have long been the most common object of study, and, as I have shown in this book, nefes are also a direction of our talk. In Bektashi society, nefes are traditionally associated with times of muhabbet. Thus the positively defined keying that I propose is that the lesson be considered a form of muhabbet. But what is muhabbet? This term was a puzzle to me for many years.

In Search of Muhabbet

in which different facets of muhabbet are presented in narratives and in explicit discussions with Baba; but it is only Baba's poetic contextualization of muhabbet in the basement kitchen that the student finally grasps

In all my years of going to the tekke, I heard continuous reference to muhabbet. But not until a year after the Hizir lesson, that is, in December 1985, did I finally feel I understood what muhabbet meant. Before then, I was trapped between two notions of muhabbet. First, with my background in Arabic, I knew that "muhabbet" was an Arabic word based on the root *hbb*, to love. Yet I also knew that in casual conversation Baba spoke of "making muhabbet" when an old friend from out of town would come to the tekke for a visit.

For years I wondered, Was muhabbet some sort of love or was it a special sort of talk? As I reflect now, it seems a foolish polarity, for certainly there can be talk with affection or talk through which affection is engendered. Perhaps it was the verb *yapmak*—to make—that was so often joined with "muhabbet" that threw me. Or perhaps it was some sort of dichotomy between feelings and actions that I was preserving. Or maybe it was a disinclination to deal with any sort of formality, which I knew existed in muhabbet, in relation to love or to talk. Whatever the case, I was effectively blinded from going beyond these distinctions. Yet what was manifestly clear from the frequency with which muhabbet came up was the importance of muhabbet in Bektashi practice.

MUHABBET LURKING IN NARRATIVES

It is not difficult to find reference to muhabbet in Baba's narratives. For example, in a narrative Baba told about the life of Ali Baba, his murshid's murshid, five of the seven episodes of the account took place in settings of muhabbet. Several of these settings illustrate the range of muhabbet—from the general to the more specifically ritual forms.

The first example shows a general sort of muhabbet. The episode occurs in the village of Haji Bektash in central Anatolia, where the *Dede*, the head of all Bektashis, used to reside.

it was the custom at Haji Bektash that the Dede~
would call all the babas to have coffee\
                          . after resting\
AND on that day too~
he had called the babas together~
and they were sitting there~
making **muhabbet**
while a dervish~ brought in the coffee~
and served them coffee in turn
                    to each so that they drink\

Muhabbet is associated here with a regular gathering during which coffee is served.

Another example of muhabbet from the same narrative is the following passage, in which a notable from the southern Albanian town of Gjirokastër, Ali Zot Bey, and his friends gather in their tekke in the evening.

... there~
... it was the custom that~
... a . group . of muhiban [1]
.. a ..... in order to make **muhabbet**~
brought themselves~
meat~ and everything necessary for a meal~
and drink and so forth
              they also used\
and~
... he
...... eh-
.... as the dervishes prepared the meal they~
they {Ali Zot Bey and company} were also drinking\
while drinking~ they drank~
and also ate\
.... while making **muhabbet**
.... a . nefes ah-
a . song {secular} .. they sang\
.... a song by the name of Fatimeh, O my flower
Ali Baba~
being a stranger thought that this~
was a nefes\
a nefes on her grace Fatimeh\ [2]

Again, muhabbet is associated with a regular gathering in a tekke, although here there is also food involved, drink that is not coffee, and singing. This example is particularly revealing, however, because it shows the link between muhabbet and nefes. This point was dramatically made in the continuing narrative when Ali Baba, who had happened in on this muhabbet, decried it as a disgraceful sort of muhabbet in a tekke setting. Ali Baba's reaction is more fully described in Baba's written account of this scene than in his spoken version. (The written account is found in Albanian in Baba's book *Misticizma Islame dhe Bektashizma* (1970). The translation below is my own.)

Babai si i riardhur dhe i huaj që ishte kur dëgjoi këngën, kujtoi se mos ishte ndonjë "nefes" për Fatimenë, të bijën e Profitit Muhammed (a.s.).

Pyeti njerëzit aty se qysh e thoshnin këtë "nefes" për këtë zonjë.

Ata i thanë:
    Jo, Baba, nuk ësht "nefes," është
    një këngë që këndohet rrugëve.

Baba Aliu u-zëmrua dhe tha:
    Oh! Qysh këngët e rugaçëve të m'i
    këndojnë mua këtu në teqe?

Dhe menjëherë mori shkopin dhe arriti atje. I
qëlloi me shko ata, u theu shishet, duke u thënë:
    Të tilla muhabete dhe të tilla
    këngë nuk i dua këtu në teqe.[3]

* * * * *

Baba, as he had recently come and was a stranger there, when he heard the song, he thought it was a nefes for Fatimeh, the daughter of the Prophet Muhammad (on whom be peace).

He asked some of them how they recited that nefes for her.

They answered,
    No Baba, this isn't a nefes, it's a song
    that's sung in the streets.

Ali Baba got angry and said,
    Oh! How can you sing a street song to
    me here in the tekke?

And immediately he grabbed a staff and stood up. He swiped at them with the staff, and broke their bottles, while calling out:
    Such muhabbet and such songs
    I will not have here in the tekke!

The baba in this passage expected the songs sung during muhabbet in the tekke to be nefes, not secular songs.

Another example of muhabbet is the one ritual time when muhabbet is especially called for. This is after the secret part of the initiation ceremony of a new muhib. The passage below, from Baba's spoken narrative on Ali Baba, describes such a time for the young Ali Baba and his best friend.

> .... later~
> evening fell~
> and they saw that there was no one\
> yet a little later still~
> they saw that two dressed as hojas~
> > in turbans~
>
> two students\
> .... had come~
> and the baba and the dervishes~
> were very pleased with them~
> that night they took their vows\
> that is~
> they "saw" the ceremony of Bektashi muhib~

{sound of prayer beads, *tesbih*, through hand of Baba}

> and they made much **muhabbet** that day~
> so~
> and they stayed for that three days~
> then they went on their way\

In his book, Baba describes this same scene in Albanian in more detail. (Note that the sacrifice of the animals can be seen to presage an initiation, for a sheep is always sacrificed for each new initiate.)

Abdullah Baba said to the dervishes,
> My sons, this evening two oil-lamps[4]
> will come as guests from Elbasan,
> so make good the preparation.
> Sacrifice two animals and make the
> dinner.

The dervishes followed the orders,
sacrificed the animals and made all ready.
The whole day passed and no one was seen.

When evening fell there appeared two
coming to the tekke, dressed as hojas.
When they (the dervishes) told the baba
of their coming, he received them with
much pleasure.

They took vows from him, and afterwards
they stayed with Abdullah Baba for three
days during which there grew a bond of
deep **affection**.

When I asked Baba about the Albanian word *dashuri*, which I have
here translated as "affection," he responded that it meant "muhabbet." On
this more explicit and conscious note, I move to Baba's explanations of
muhabbet in and beyond the lessons.

"Why Do You Flee This Muhabbet?"

In the above passages from the narrative on Ali Baba, muhabbet was presented as a general form of congenial social interaction, as a sort of gathering in which talk, and sometimes food, drink, and song prevailed, and
where, if the setting was a tekke, nefes were the appropriate song. Muhabbet was also presented as the more public ceremony after the secret part
of the initiation ceremony of a muhib at the tekke. However, in none of
these examples of scenes of muhabbet did the muhabbet itself stand out.
Rather, what stood out in these narratives was the dramatic action. The
setting was just that—a background.

More to the fore, muhabbet was an actual topic of discussion in several lessons. The earliest one of these discussions that I have on tape occurred in June 1985, a month before Baba's narrative on Ali Baba, and five
months before the Hizir lesson. If teaching is to be evaluated by the recall
of the student, however, then Baba's explanations in these discussions were
most unsuccessful. I had no recollection of them; I had not even noted the
explanations in my index of topics covered in particular tapes and only
stumbled upon them when listening to the earliest tapes in an attempt to
understand how taping of lessons evolved. It seems that, as with muhabbet

in the narratives, Baba's explanations of muhabbet faded into the background of the particular texts—a poetic text in the first explanation and a narrative one in the second—with which Baba closed his explanations.

Although Baba's explanations did not initially lead to any insight on my part, they do provide testimony to my early interest in *muhabbet* and they contrast with Baba's later poetic contextualization of muhabbet which finally registered.

The context of Baba's first explanation of muhabbet in the taped lessons took place after a brief discussion of differences in regional singing in Albania. I innocently asked, using an Albanian word for "song" that implied a secular song:

tekkede çok kënge söyliyorlardı?

* * * * *

in the tekke were many songs sung?

Baba's response to my question about secular songs in the tekke was first to correct my reference to secular songs to nefes and gazel.[5] Then he gave an example of how these sounded, by chanting several lines from a nefes by Fuzuli (sixteenth century).

> Beni candan usandırdı
> Cefadan yar usanmaz mı
> Felekler yandı ahımdan

> * * * * *

> She/he exhausted me to the soul
> Does my Beloved never tire of torture
> The heavens were set afire from my moanings

But as it was Ramadan and he was fasting, Baba's voice then gave out. I told him I would ask for the rest of this nefes when he was feeling stronger, but I had become intrigued and asked:

how was the custom~
of chanting nefes~

of making muhabbet~
how was the custom
        at the tekke
            in Albania?

To ask this I must have had some sense of the important connection between nefes and muhabbet.

Baba answered that first the dervishes and muhiban at the tekke in Albania would enter into the *namaz*, the worship through prayer, and then when prayers were over, they would gather around the table, and there at the table muhabbet would take place. They would begin drinking, and the baba would start with a gazel, then the others would sing a gazel. At this point Baba asked if I had not yet seen how they did it there at the Michigan tekke. He then assured me that the next time someone took vows (the most predictable time of muhabbet) he would call me for the muhabbet.

I asked whether muhabbet always took place in the evening, which set Baba off on describing how it proceeds in Michigan. He described how the others use alcoholic drink, while he has a Coke or a Pepsi. (In Albania, some tekkes permitted alcohol, whereas Ali Baba's, which was also Baba's, did not. This issue is traced back to the Qur'an, which is often interpreted as proscribing alcoholic drink. Baba interprets the Qur'an as proscribing drunkeness, but not alcohol per se, although as an example he does not indulge.) Baba continued by saying that he had made a practice of opening the muhabbet by reciting an Albanian nefes by Naim Frashëri,[6] a nineteenth-century Albanian poet whom Baba later quoted on pantheism in the Hizir lesson. Despite the earlier weakness of his voice, Baba chanted the nefes for me, which led to the closing of the lesson. The part of the lesson that stayed in my memory, though, was the nefes by Frashëri, not Baba's description of muhabbet.

The following week I opened the taping by asking Baba about muhabbet. Unlike the preceding week when I had asked about the custom or tradition of muhabbet, this time I asked about the meaning of the custom as well. Baba's explanation, although it did not stay with me then, makes it very clear that it was in sessions of muhabbet that much Bektashi teaching took place.

Baba: the purpose of muhabbet
    .. was to teach the talib or murids {another term for talib}\

...... that is, so that the talib learn
what it is
.. the essentials of the Order~
.. the bases of the Order~
the Order's
...... inner meaning\
FT: yes
Baba: in "sessions" of muhabbet~
..... all the people would gather~
.... all the murids~   {talib}
.... all the aşıks~ [7]
and they would speak together muhabbet\
while conversing~
.. they would start up with a nefes
FT: hmm
Baba: of one of the poets
.... Baba himself would chant it first
a nefes\
and then he would explain that nefes~
.... uh- what was its point~
of the nefes~
what did it say\
FT: yes
Baba: that is~
was it to respond to the murshid~
.... was it to praise the murshid?
... of what the murshid was~
that is~
the feelings~
about feelings toward the murshid~
how to explain these feelings~
how they were said~
to what compared-
to a beautiful beloved?
something like that~
so that later they understood what was
the essential meaning\
FT: yes
Baba: thus it is\
this is the wisdom\

FT: yes
Baba: the muhabbet would
   continue\
   then they would all recite another poem\
   and another meaning would come out\
   for example~
   what was in the Order~
   what were the ways of the Order~
   why did they do it that way~
   and so forth~
   and say it that way\
   the special ways would all be explained~
   there~
   in the making of muhabbet\
   so that the meaning of muhabbet was this~
   came out this way~
   to .. to make the murids {talibs} "ripen"

I announced that I understood, which if true was a fleeting experience, and then I asked if muhabbet was done that way in Albania. Baba responded by describing again the gathering for muhabbet after the prayers and the baba starting off with a nefes or a story. Then Baba himself broke into such a story—one that his murshid, Selim Baba, had been especially fond of telling during muhabbet. The story was the narrative of Hizir and Musa.

Baba explained first that the purpose of this story was to teach the importance of submission by the talib to the murshid, and of the caliber of trust that was expected. In this telling, unlike the account in the Hizir lesson five months later, Baba relayed only the first incident about Hizir pounding holes in the boat and Musa being unable to restrain himself from remarking on this. Then Baba quoted a line in Arabic from the Qur'an about lack of patience, and the lesson ended. As in the previous week's lesson, what stayed in my mind was the text, here of Musa and Hizir, there the poem by Naim (Frashëri). Baba's clear elucidations of muhabbet did not stick.

Then a full year and a half later, on December 12, 1986, we were gathered around the table in the basement kitchen, where we had just finished a meal of egg-lemon soup, chicken, potatoes and carrots, and watermelon—watermelon in December! We sat there talking and the dervish brought us coffee. No one wanted to leave.

That week Baba had returned from the hospital where he had earlier been taken in a greatly weakened state. While he was gone a muhib had begun praying for Baba at the as-yet-unfinished *türbe* (the mausoleum for Baba on tekke grounds). Even though Baba had come back to the tekke the day before, the muhib, who worked the evening shift, had still come at 3 a.m. to pray. He had come later that morning again to check on Baba, and when asked why he had come the night before, he explained that he had done so to give thanks for Baba's recovery. Baba's sister, Zonja Zejnep, then remarked that the türbe would be like the Ka'aba—the sacred black stone in Mecca (i.e., a place of pilgrimage).

At the table for lunch, Baba sat at the head as usual; Zoti Ago, the tall aristocrat from coastal Albania, to his right; Zonja Zejnep to his right; followed by the dervish and Zoti Fadil, the cook. On the other side of the table, I was at Baba's left, with the brother-in-law of the muhib who had prayed at the türbe next to me, then Suriyye, the wife of that muhip, and then Zoti Myrto, who also lived at the tekke and helped with driving and many other tasks.

We did not often sit for coffee after a meal, but that day, as I mentioned, no one wanted to leave. Zoti Ago and I were talking about Albanian grammar, in particular about case endings and then the admirative mood, which is a full conjugation used especially to show surprise. This feature is an object of pride, for Albanians recognize that most languages are not so endowed.

I mentioned that I had trouble keeping all this Albanian in my head, to which Zoti Ago facetiously but playfully suggested memory medicine. The topic shifted to dialects and how in Baba's dialect speakers use what should be a masculine ending on feminine words. Zoti Ago, who is not from Baba's region, gave an example of this masculine ending on Zonja Zejnep's name. It sounded fine to me and I remarked as such, to which Zoti Ago exploded, "Teach her Albanian!" Baba responded that no, he would teach me Gjirokastri, his dialect.

I asked Zoti Ago about his dialect and he gave examples showing how he did not palatalize his velars. Then we got to talking about where people's families came from. Baba's father's family had originally come from Gjakova in what is now Yugoslavia, had then gone to Elbasan in central Albania, and finally to Gjirokastër, or Ergeri as the Turks called it, in southern Albania. Zoti Ago noted that people from Gjirokastër were strange, that they all married their cousins and were incestuous. That's why they were alike in appearance and speech. It was clear that Zoti Ago was happy to have Baba back.

When I asked where Zoti Ago's family came from, he replied that they came from the north of Albania, but exactly where, only God knew. Somehow we got to telling stories, with Zoti Ago telling of two sisters, one of whom married a man with a kettleful of gold, while her sister married a poor villager. Yet when the wealthy husband was later shot, he was killed by one so poor that after the second shot the killer pulled off a button and used it as the next bullet. (It is possible I missed something in the Albanian.) This account was all part of the dirge with which the wife of the rich man mourned him.

Zoti Ago then described how when he was little, he remembered the women in villages coming out in a line to mourn when someone died, and of how they grieved in poetry. This poetry included praise of the dead, curses for the killer or cause of death, and verses about the grief of the family. Once when the praise had gotten out of hand, one woman had even been heard to overtly reprimand the others, saying that they should not praise the dead man so highly but rather tell of him as he had been.

I told a story of when I was in a village in southern Lebanon and a man died and the women sang at his funeral. They sang of him as if he were still a young man, but I had sat with him the week before his death, when he had showed me how to roll cigarettes, and he was seventy if he was a day. Zoti Ago asked if the old hadn't any importance. And then I told of a fifteen-year-old student of mine who had died in a village in Lebanon, and how the women had done slow wedding dances and sung of him as if he were a groom, for he had never been married and so needed to be sung through the life he had missed.

At this the family of the muhib who had prayed for Baba joined in, recounting how the women in Albania chanted the dirges, how they composed the *vajtimi*. Suriyye said that it was the women, not the men, who could do this rhymed singing. Her brother noted, "Over there we cried in poetry."

But do not think this talk of dirges was only somber. Like the earlier talk about dialect and families, singing for the dead was a most democratic of topics, for, as with dialect and family, all could share in it. And the talk of death, with Baba so recently returned, was not so much a veiled reference as a unifying theme. For, as with other Balkan peoples, the Albanians seem to have a predisposition to tragedy, and what they sing of, they experience, and what they experience, they sing of, and never do they seem more together than when talking of death.

Zoti Ago continued by recalling how the untutored village women sang the best dirges, and he even let loose a verse in his deep baritone voice, something about a dove. This was discussed and some archaic words were explained. Then, because the poetry had begun, I contributed several Albanian poems Baba had taught me: one about the end of winter, and one of love for a city in central Albania.

But it was getting on in time and I said I would have to return to Ann Arbor. Baba looked at me, lowered his eyelids, and chanted the final quatrain from the sixteenth-century nefes by Pir Sultan Abdal:

> Pir Sultanım kani yüksek uçarsın
> Selamsız sabahsız gelir geçersin
> **Güzel muhabbetten niçin kaçarsın?**
> Böyle mıdır yolumuzun turağsı[8]
>
> Böyle mıdır yolumuzun turağsı huuu

And then I knew. Then I knew what muhabbet was. The third line was what Baba was singling out.

> Güzel muhabbetten niçin kaçarsın?

* * * * *

> Why do you flee this touching muhabbet?

Why did I have to leave this muhabbet?

There was no explanation that could reach as this did. For what Baba did by singing of muhabbet during a time of muhabbet was name the closeness and pleasure and joy we were having in each other's company, in our muhabbet.

As Annie Sullivan had put Helen Keller's hand under the water pump and, with the water pouring out, finger-spelled "water" into her hand, so Baba had song-spelled "muhabbet" for me with muhabbet washing over us in the basement kitchen of the tekke.

VI. Learning as Attunement

My sudden understanding of muhabbet through Baba's poetic naming of it in the tekke's basement kitchen led me to rethink Baba's and my lessons that had taken place in the room above the kitchen for the past fifteen years. The lessons, too, were times of muhabbet!

Many features of the lessons that had unsettled and confused me—the lack of syllabus, of directives, of overt evaluation or correction, the wide range and fluidity of reference, and even the pleasure and humor that were so much a part of the lessons—all of these aspects were consistent with muhabbet as it takes place after private rituals at the tekke. There Baba chants a spiritual poem or nefes and is followed by others who chant what nefes they choose. Sometimes there is discussion with Baba explaining references in the nefes, but always there is a sense of relaxed give and take. As Baba described muhabbet in a lesson that took place a month after his basement contextualization:

> muhabbet is~
> a sort of praise or remembrance of God~
> to soften the heart and cleanse the conscience\
> in beautiful muhabbet~
> the beautiful recitations of nefes
> work for the spiritual enlightenment\
> in listening~
> listeners become cleansed in their hearts and consciences\

I consider the recasting of Baba's and my interaction from the frame of "lessons" to the frame of muhabbet as the meta-attunement of the study. More common forms of attunement in the study have included conventions of opening and closing episodes within lessons, the connecting of narratives across lessons, and the drift toward the language of nefes.

In this final chapter I review different forms and figures of attunement that have been described in the study. First, though, I recall the basic questions and early analogies that led to the positing of attunement as a way to describe the teaching and learning of murshid and talib. Then, just as I opened the study with a description of a question to Baba—"Baba, how did Selim Baba teach you?"—I will close with description of another question to Baba. This second question shows progression in my understanding of the nature of our lessons.

At the end of the book is an epilogue. It is a story that Baba has told me several times and that comes from the thirteenth-century murshid Rumi. In this story, Rumi conveys in one page what I have taken many to suggest.

Forms of Figures of Attunement

> in which the student takes the reader backstage to reveal the backdrop of thought, followed by a fast-forwarding of definitions and forms of attunement in somewhat tedious but summary fashion

The basic question of this book is how a talib learns with the murshid or "spiritual master" in the context of dialogues in an Islamic monastery. This question can be phrased more personally, because I have been studying with a Bektashi murshid for over fifteen years now. What then has been going on during our lessons together?

My assumption was that a description of a lesson with Baba would shed most light on the murshid-talib relationship, but I was faced with the puzzle of how to view the relationship of murshid and talib in the context of analyzing a lesson. Previous Islamic studies have preserved the poetry of murshids and certain biographical details but have tended to take for granted the process of their teaching.[1] Previous interactional studies, such as those between interviewer and client, teacher and student, or doctor and patient, have also taken the relationships for granted. Other discourse studies have tended to fossilize transcriptions of interaction, whereas in the case of Baba and myself, if learning indeed took place, a developmental approach was necessary.

This is not to say that Islamic, interactional, and discourse studies were not later useful, but that they did not prove helpful in basic thinking about the relationship. So I took a different tack and reflected on what relationship in the America that I knew was closest to the murshid-talib relationship as I had experienced it.

Through discussions with friends, the relationship of Annie Sullivan and Helen Keller[2] was the best parallel I found.[3] Like the traditional murshid-talib relationship, Annie Sullivan and Helen Keller's was for life, and it was a relationship enhanced by intense loyalty and love. And just as the murshid is the way for the talib to come into spiritual knowledge, so Annie Sullivan provided the way for Helen Keller to come into knowledge of the verbal world. Both Annie Sullivan and the murshid then led their students to new ways of perceiving.

I found another stimulating parallel in Bambi Schieffelin's (1981) study on the learning of the "ade" relationship,[4] a special relationship of brother and sister among the Kaluli people of Papua New Guinea. Her essay is a sort of child language-acquisition study that documented a mother's teaching her young daughter how to respond to her brother in the context of their special relationship.

The language learning in the relationship of Annie Sullivan and Helen Keller and in the New Guinea relationship helped me conceive of the murshid-talib relationship in similar terms. The parallel fit well because language has played such an important role in Baba's lessons with me—in our give and take, in his narratives, and in our reciting of nefes. Thus the basic analogy of the study evolved into another form: the learning in the relationship of talib to murshid was like the learning of a language, with language understood as personally linked games whose main game is the sharing of nefes, and whose linkages have theological significance.

Although the mother-child relationship common to many studies of child language-acquisition is not the first parallel that comes to mind in the picture of me in my folding chair and Baba in his high-back one in the tekke study room, there are important similarities with the murshid-talib relationship. In both the mother-child relationship of child language-acquisition studies and the murshid-talib relationship, dialogue is important. Both are nurturing relationships in which there are repeated affirmations of the relationship; and just as the mother is seen as crucial in the one, so the murshid is seen as crucial in the other. Furthermore, the mother's grasp of the language and ways of the society far exceeds that of the child, as the murshid's experience in spiritual matters exceeds that of the talib. This differential is used not to tyrannize, however, but to foster a direction in communication toward the ways of the mother or the ways of the murshid. In this process, language is passed on, as is the relationship.

The direction of the lessons toward the language of nefes was a development of the basic analogy that the murshid-talib interaction was one of language learning and the relationship was like that of mother and child in language-acquisition studies. But where does "attunement" fit in?

The notion of attunement evolved from the challenge to describe the interaction of Baba and myself in our lessons that I had taped between 1985 and 1987. I mention the dates to emphasize my focus on actual transcripts of lessons. The most intriguing aspect about these exchanges was the way Baba appeared to sit back. Despite his unquestioned authority in spiritual matters, Baba never initiated lessons, never issued directives, never appeared even to correct me. There was no outside syllabus that I could recognize. Instead I was left to initiate discussion.

In addition to this apparent power vacuum, there was also a great range and fluidity of reference, as well as laughter and pleasure, even about matters of deep concern. For those who know the Bektashis, the laughter is no surprise because in the Ottoman context Bektashis were well known for their humor and for their delight in poking fun at legalistic forms of Islam. But when I asked Baba to characterize his Order, he responded:

we would never pull the veil~
from anyone's face\

I was taken aback by this response. I had expected some theological point of difference with Sunni practice, or mention of the wide social range of membership, or some humorous anecdote. Instead Baba affirmed a basic respect for human dignity. (Despite the Islamic context, the "veil" that Baba referred to has nothing to do with sexual modesty. It should be noted again that the Bektashi sense of human dignity extends to women. Bektashis have accepted and initiated women as inner members since the beginning of the Order in central Anatolia more than seven hundred years ago. This acceptance of women has brought them criticism over the centuries and yet they have persisted in it. The current Bektashis' acceptance of me as Baba's student was certainly facilitated by the long-standing precedent of female talibs.)

In the context of murshid-talib relations I interpret Baba's response of never pulling the veil from anyone's face to mean that teaching should be accomplished with careful respect for the learner, which in turn suggests that description of Baba's teaching is no simple matter. What proved most useful in defining this process, though, was not role delineation but development of interaction across the lesson. That is, despite the appearance that the wrong person was taking the initiatives, and despite the wide range of reference and variety of verbal play that Baba and I engaged in, there still appeared to be a direction in our lessons—to better questions on my part, to greater resonance of narratives, to greater prominence of nefes, and throughout to the continual affirmation of Baba's and my relationship. This drift was not a development in a logical sense, but nonetheless there was a development, and it is this quality that I labeled "attunement."

I have described attunement in many ways in the book: through negative analogy, through positive definition, and through a multitude of examples. The point of all these descriptions was to try to characterize Baba's and my interaction from a variety of perspectives.

A negative analogy to attunement was presented in the contrast between the professor's interview with Baba and the Hizir lesson. The interview was choppier, both in terms of frequency of questioning and number of episodes, than the most question-filled of my lessons. More significantly, Baba's responses in the interview became shorter and shorter, and his irritation grew, until verbal interaction ceased. In contrast, the Hizir lesson lasted for seventy minutes, and was ended only by outside interruption. The interaction constantly built on and resonated with earlier interactions. But to belabor the contrast of interview and lesson is to come dangerously close to violating the principle of another's veil.

I also described attunement by defining it positively as "an increasing coordination through play-full recollecting of dialogue with another." This definition implies that Baba and I get better at playing verbal games with each other, the more shared experiences we had to build on. It also implies that our subtlety and collusion similarly increased, and that the stuff of our play was memories.

In my initial definition, though, I left "increasing coordination" unspecified. What is it that is becoming coordinated? "Verbal repertoire" is a partial answer. In other words, attunement is an increasing coordination of verbal repertoire, but that is not all. It is worth noting here that an earlier title of this book was "Tuning the Heart." My intention was to convey that attunement of murshid and talib is also an increasing coordination of the heart of the talib and murshid, with "heart" understood as the seat of higher faculties of perception. Murshids inspire devotion in their talibs. In our American society one would not continue voluntarily to meet weekly with another person if the care for that other were not strong.[5] Furthermore, "tuning the heart" also applies beyond the relationship with the murshid, for discussion with Baba relates to questions of God, His servants, and His creation.

In addition to negative analogy and positive definition, I have offered many examples of attunement in Baba's and my interaction. The first example of attunement that I gave was of my understanding of "hu." For many years, although I knew "hu" came from the third-person singular Arabic pronoun for "he," I assumed its use and therefore meaning to be similar to "amen." Then one day when reading to Baba I suddenly recognized "hu" in places I had never noticed it before, leading to my new understanding that "hu" was both a name of God, in the Muslim sense that God is referred to by "hu" ("He") in the Qur'an, and that it can refer indirectly as well to one's murshid. Truly a pronoun of the heart.

Like my sudden understanding of muhabbet through Baba's poetic naming in the basement kitchen, my re-understanding of "hu" had been a sort of swift illumination. Despite the dramatic quality of these experiences, they were based on much previous contact both with the terms and with the illuminator. As Harriet Feinberg noted in her study of teaching and learning in Martin Buber's *Hasidic Tales* (1972), sudden illumination depends on a shared reference system of teacher and student and on spiritual strength built up over long periods of interaction. I repeat this example in detail to emphasize the innumerable instances of my previous contact with "hu" and "muhabbet" before broader understanding was reached. Most other examples of attunement are less dramatic, but they depend no less on numerous previous contacts.

The first large grouping of forms of attunement in the study were those that can be related to the structure of Baba's and my interaction. The other grouping of forms of attunement were those that were finer, and related more to the texture of our interaction. Both sorts are also forms of cohesion of the interaction as text, and of the interactants.

In looking at the structure of Baba's and my lessons, I defined the episode as a basic unit whose brackets were negotiated but at the same time conventionalized by long interaction (first figure).

Figure of Attunement: Structure of an Episode

Opening sequence
　　my reference
　　　　　　$\longrightarrow$ Baba's response
　　　　　　　　　　$\longrightarrow$ my reference
　　　　　　　　　　　　(transition)

Body
　　Baba's response

Closing sequence
    Baba's initiation of closure, commonly with discourse marker "işte"
        ⟶ my affirmation
                ⟶ Baba's confirmation

An example of attunement across openings occurred in the latter episodes of the Hizir lesson, all centering on Baba Bayram, in which my questions led to completion of the pattern of the Bektashi clerical hierarchy in the narrative. Examples of attunement in closings were the instances when I voiced affirmation to Baba's initiation of closure in aphoristic form, a form which showed elementary reach to a Bektashi form of expression. Baba's ensuing confirmations were in the quintessential Bektashi form, the nefes. A figure of attunement that I projected from this is shown in the second figure.

Figure of Attunement: Drift to Nefes

reference
    ⟶ response

        reference based on interaction
           ⟶ response toward Bektashi form

        nefes
           ⟶ nefes

I refer to this figure as a projection: we never got to the point of exchanging nefes for nefes in the Hizir lesson, though in later lessons we did. These exchanges were not previously brought up in the study because they took place well after the Hizir lesson, but I mention them here to support the contention that there is a drift toward the language of nefes.

    The lessons in which Baba and I moved into the game of reciting nefes back and forth to each other, much like the events in the evening muhabbet, occurred in lessons after Baba's basement contextualization of muhabbet. In these lessons I had begun to treat nefes differently. By contextualizing muhabbet for me in a way that I could finally grasp, Baba had spoken to me through the nefes. That particular nefes would always be personally meaningful to me. By speaking in such an utterly memorable way with a nefes,[6] Baba had made even more clear the possibility of our communicating similarly with other nefes.

So where our lessons in the past had been a medley of readings of nefes, of Baba's telling stories, of discussion of holidays and love of God and metrics and whatever, after Baba's contextualization of muhabbet this hodge-podge continued but we gradually began to focus more on particular nefes and I began to memorize them. This led in turn to Baba talking more personally about his love of certain lines of nefes, and to a new game wherein one of us recited a quatrain and the other picked up and responded by reciting the following quatrain of the same nefes. It also led to my being able to voice affirmations of understanding in terms of nefes.

For example, in the nefes by Pir Sultan Abdal that I have quoted so often in this study, the fourth quatrain is:

> Didar muhabbet'le doyulmaz
> Mahabbetten kaçan insan sayılmaz
> Münkir üflemekle çırag söyünmez
> Tutuşunca yanar aşkın çırası.

* * * * *

> Love is not fulfilled with glances,
> **Who flees from love is not a man.**[7]
> The candle {talib} is not put out by the breath of a denier.
> Once afire, the light of passion burns.

In discussing the second line of this stanza, Baba made clear that one of the defining distinctions of humans is that humans know where they come from and where they go, whereas animals only come, eat, drink, do what they will, and then depart. I responded to this that yes, I had understood as much. Then as evidence of my understanding I quoted a line:

> Nerden gelüp gittiğini
> anlamayan hayvan imiş

* * * * *

> Where one has come from and whither goes,
> who understands this not is but an animal

This line is from the nefes by Niyazi Mısri that Baba had quoted more than a year before in the Hizir lesson (see Appendix B for the full text in Turkish). In the fourth episode of the Hizir lesson, Baba had quoted from this nefes to the effect that one should not go with just any murshid, but only with the perfected murshid, "murshid-i kâmil." My above quotation was from two stanzas earlier in the nefes. This quoting was a sure sign of my understanding not only of Baba's point in elucidating the line from the Pir Sultan Abdal nefes, but also of how Bektashis have spoken of this understanding.

Baba's response to my recitation was to join in on the last words of the line, and then to assert, "Why most certainly." And certainly my re-membering the line from the nefes and then reciting it as an affirmation in our lesson was an attunement—a playful recollecting of earlier dialogues with Baba.

Another figure of attunement during the Hizir lesson that supports the drift toward the language of nefes is the gradual surfacing of nefes by Baba in the lesson. That is, Baba responds by bringing up nefes earlier and earlier in episodes as the lesson progresses. This tendency can be seen as a sign that my episode-initiating references are coming closer to questions that Bektashis have traditionally been concerned with. This progression stops, however, when I am unable to follow Baba's point about a nefes being written in circles on the page. The third figure summarizes the gradual surfacing of nefes in the Hizir lesson.

Figure of Attunement: Gradual Surfacing of Nefes Across a Lesson

1st episode: at close, my aphoristic statement and Baba's

    4th episode: at close, my aphoristic statement, nefes by Baba

       6th episode: nefes behind whole episode

          7th episode: at outset, nefes by Baba in response to my
               initiating question

Within the grouping of structurally related forms of attunement, but more idiosyncratic than the previous examples, are forms of attunement by Baba and myself that show a righting of our relationship after some affront or variation. The main example from the Hizir lesson was the gross change of format, from a more interviewlike interaction in the first seven episodes to our more usual form of interaction in the last four episodes. A sketch of this attunement is shown in the fourth figure.

Figure of Attunement: Gross Change of Format Across a Lesson

(episodes 1 to 7)
interviewlike
multiple shifts of direction of discussion
reference to project outside lesson (i.e., dissertation)

⟶

(episodes 8 to 11)
usual interaction between Baba and me
continuous direction of discussion in narrative
total demise of reference to dissertation

Turning to the other main grouping of forms of attunement—that is, of those I described as nonstructural and textural—I presented how Baba and I played on each other's languages in terms of native languages, dialect, and syntax, leading to what I called "attunement slides." Attunement slides are passages where Baba and I drew on each other's language so closely that it appeared that we were predicting, correctly, the other's words and phrases. Again, this would only be possible with people who have interacted over a long period of time.

I also described how retellings of narratives are a sort of play into the syntax of the memory of the talib and a powerful tool of communication. I closed my discussion of these more delicate forms of attunement by tracing Baba's teaching of the word "sophistry" across the lesson. He used it, then recognized that I had not followed him. So he defined the word and soon after modified a nefes to include the new word in the verse. When several episodes later he used the word again, humorously, there was no question. It was securely in my repertoire.

Besides tracing the teaching of "sophistry" I also traced Baba's knitting up of the lesson through confirmations that both closed episodes and celebrated Baba's and my initial coming together for study.

It is from this section about more delicate attunements that I presented an answer to the question of how Baba teaches. Earlier I had said that it appeared Baba taught through strategies that facilitated periodic and more far-reaching attunement. By the end of my study I was able to simplify this propositon. By then it appeared that Baba taught through constantly drawing playful connections in our talk, so much so that I could not but join in. And these connections reached to the playful dialogue he had shared with his murshid, who had shared with his murshid, and so on back in time.

The Walls of the Lesson

in which the student once again recognizes sore limitations in her mind-set

"Baba, where in the tekke did Selim Baba teach you?" A simple enough question, but it had taken years until I knew enough to ask it.

Not only had it taken years of study with Baba, but it had also taken Baba's contextualization of muhabbet in the basement kitchen. Only after I knew muhabbet from named experience did I have the sense to ask the question of where in the tekke in Albania Baba had been taught. Baba's answer confirmed my conclusion that our lessons were a form of muhabbet. But if the lessons were a form of muhabbet, why had it taken me so long to see this? One answer that I have already given is that I had trouble "seeing" muhabbet. Yet even if I had understood the emotional and social setting of muhabbet sooner, there was still an impediment, a wall to my linking the interaction of our lessons with the interaction of sessions of muhabbet.

The highest "wall" blocking my understanding was my assumption that we regularly had a lesson. I held to this assumption, despite the fact that Baba's and my interaction did not fit my model of a lesson. This obstinacy on my part was reflected in and reinforced by my translation of *ders*. Both Baba and I referred to our time together upstairs as "ders," and Baba playfully called the room the "dershane." In my mind I translated "ders" as "lesson" and "dershane" as "classroom." But "ders" in Turkish or Arabic can also be translated "study," with a "dershane," or "study room." The softening from the implications of "lesson" to "study" leads away from popular Western frame-words of classroom learning. But it is still a long way from muhabbet.

It was not until Baba had contextualized muhabbet for me in the basement kitchen, and I had learned some nefes and had participated in muhabbet in the basement meeting room, that I was able to ask the more critical question—"Baba, *where* did Selim Baba teach you?"

Baba described how the road leading to his tekke in Albania was lined with poplar trees. Past the trees there was a big, stone gate that was always open. Outside the gate there were some tombstones of previous dervishes with their distinctive headgear fashioned in stone on the top of the markers. Inside the gate there was a large courtyard. There, were more tombstones: one of the founder of the tekke, and the other of Ali Baba, Baba's murshid's murshid.

The tekke complex itself included three main buildings. To the left was the guest house, where guests and dervishes slept. The middle building contained the kitchen and eating room. Behind that was where the animals were kept. And to the right was the building where the baba of the tekke slept and worked and prayed. The baba's room was a large one. Down the hall, in a little room Baba Rexheb (then Dervish Rexheb) lived, for he was the baba's personal assistant. Also in this building was the *meydan*, the private ceremonial room, with an additional room for the person in charge of the meydan.

Of these rooms, it is the baba's room that is the most important. As I mentioned, it was large. Or, as Baba put it, it was long enough for a line of fifty men to bow, kneel, and say their prayers from end to end. There the baba slept, carried on his correspondence, studied his books, and greeted and entertained guests. And there muhabbet was held. This was also where Selim Baba taught Baba; thus the study room and the room of muhabbet were one.

In contrast, at the tekke in Michigan, Baba's bedroom is separate from the greeting room, which is separate from the study room. As for muhabbet, it is held far away on a different floor in the basement. This separation of activities that the small rooms of the old Michigan farmhouse necessitated was something I took for granted. The lessons or study were in a separate room from Baba's in the tekke, so I kept them distant also in my mind.

It was only as I understood more and more the importance of nefes in the lessons and the drift of our talk toward nefes, and only after Baba had "named" muhabbet for me in a setting of muhabbet, that I was able to see a connection. Only then was I able to question my assumption of the separation of study and muhabbet.

Cross-cultural attunement over time cannot but lead to the questioning of walls of our minds, including most profoundly the settings of how and where we learn.

Epilogue

in which the student follows the master through the streets and achieves attunement in a most precarious fashion

Baba has several times told me a story of the famous Sufi, Jelaleddin Rumi of Konya, and his murshid, Shemseddin Tabrizi.

It seems that one day Rumi went to his murshid's house. But when he arrived, he found that Tabrizi had just left. Rumi quickly looked down the narrow streets and saw the coattails of his master as he turned into an alley. He followed his murshid. Yet whenever he got near, Tabrizi was just turning another corner in the twisting streets. Finally Tabrizi went into a house, and Rumi followed him in. But once inside he did not see his master anywhere, so he went up on the flat roof. But he did not see him on the roof, either.

So he jumped off, and his murshid caught him in his arms.

Notes

Prologue

1. Obviously "monastery" is a Christian term, but the Bektashis in America use it for want of a better word when describing their Muslim center, their *tekke*, in English. Still, once the Islamic nature of the tekke is clear, to refer to it as a monastery is not totally misleading. In particular, Baba and the other cleric, the dervish, are both celibate. Bektashism has two branches: one celibate, the other noncelibate. Among Albanians the celibate branch has always had the greater respect. Another similarity to a monastery is that Baba and the dervish live at the tekke full time, and guests can come and stay there.

Unlike most monasteries, however, the tekke has a membership of initiated members (*muhiban*), both male and female, who live with their own families outside the tekke but who come regularly to the tekke for private ritual worship. The tekke also has a membership of people who are not initiated but who are drawn to the baba (*aşıklar*) and who come to see Baba and attend public ceremonies. There are other family members of the muhiban and the aşıklar who also attend public ceremonies and may come to the tekke for prayers or merely company. Thus the tekke is much more a community center than are most monasteries.

2. The best source on Bektashism is still John Kingsley Birge's *The Bektashi Order of Dervishes* (1937), the research for which was done in Turkey and Albania in the late 1920s. The Bektashis were one of the two main Sufi Orders of the Ottoman Empire, the other being the better known Mevlevi Order, also known as the "whirling dervishes." In Ottoman history, the Bektashis were known for their connection with the Janissaries, the elite troops of the empire. Bektashis traveled with the troops in a sort of chaplain-missionary role. Bektashis were also known for their humor and their gentle deriding of the more legalistic Sunni or orthodox Muslims.

3. The Arabic-based Persian term for "inner members" is *muhiban*. It is a feature of Sufi Orders that the muhiban, who live outside the tekke, are important members. Whereas other Orders have accepted women members only sometimes, the Bektashis are known for their continued acceptance of women as initiated members from the inception of their Order. This has meant that women have long participated in the tekke's private ritual that was closed to everyone except other initiated members. In the Ottoman Empire this was most unusual, for the inclusion of women provoked a situation that was already ripe for gossip. Non-Bektashis did not realize, however, that when a woman was initiated the other people she was initiated with became her brothers and sisters. Thus she always had

the protection in the private ritual that biological brothers would have accorded in public. Indeed, an initiated Bektashi woman is known as *baci* or "sister." She also could not be initiated with her husband, for then, as he had become a brother, they could no longer be married.

4. Celibacy is unusual in Islam, but since the reorganization of Bektashism in the 1500s by Balim Sultan there has been a highly regarded celibate branch. Once a young Muslim Arab-American visitor queried Baba on this point, noting that the Qur'an commanded Muslims to be fruitful and multiply. Baba answered back, more sharply than usual, "Do you think all children are children of the flesh?" Indeed, all people who come to the tekke are seen as Baba's children. My particular title there is the southern Albanian word for "daughter of Baba."

5. Turkish is native to neither Baba nor myself, but it has long been our language of communication. Baba learned Turkish first in elementary school in Albania, for in the early part of this century Albania was still a part of the Ottoman Empire. Baba also studied and used Turkish in the Bektashi tekkes in Albania and Egypt because Turkish has long been the main language of the Bektashis. I first studied Turkish at age nineteen, later spent time in Turkey, and then majored in Turkish for undergraduate and graduate degrees in Near Eastern Languages and Literature at the University of Michigan. But it is the years of weekly sessions in Turkish with Baba that have made the language our own.

Chapter I: Introduction

1. *Halife* comes from the Arabic *khalifa*, signifying "successor" as in "successor to the leadership of the Islamic community." The equivalent Western term is "caliph." In Bektashi hierarchy (muhib, dervish, baba, halife, dede), halife is the next-to-highest position, and could be likened to a bishop in the Anglican Church. The most important power of a halife is that he can perform the ritual to make a dervish a baba.

2. The talib is supposed to stay with the murshid until the murshid dies. At that time the talib would be responsible for the murshid's poetry, to disseminate or publish it. Baba's problem was that he had to flee for his life from the Communists, against whom at his murshid's bidding he had been working. He could not know he would never see his murshid again and that Albania would be closed to him for almost fifty years.

3. According to Islamic tradition, Muhammad received the Qur'an from God through the Angel Gabriel.

4. "Imams" here refers to the twelve imams or Muslim religious leaders who were of the Prophet's family, and who are recognized by Shi'a Muslims as the legitimate successors to the Prophet.

5. Harriet Feinberg (1972), 189. Courtney Cazden called this text to my attention, for which I am most grateful.

6. A chronogram is a phrase or a poetic line, the sum of the numerical value of whose letters equals a relevant date. In the chronogram in question, the alphabet is the Arabic one, and the sum is the date of Baba's birth.

7. Frances Trix (1984), "What's in a Naming? Discourse Analysis Through Multiple Frames of an Islamic Lesson" (unpublished qualifying paper, Linguistics Department, University of Michigan), fall 1984.

8. All the other major Islamic holidays—*aid al-adha* (the sacrifice holiday), *aid al-fitr* (the holiday of breaking of the fast), and *Ashura* (commemorating the martyrdom of Husein at Kerbela)—are lunar-based; that is, they occur according to a lunar-based calendar. In relation to the solar calendar in general Western use, it appears as if these Muslim holidays occur earlier each year. In approximately forty years, they make a complete rotation of the solar calendar.

In contrast, *Nevruz*, as the Turks call it, is the one major Islamic holiday that occurs on the same day according to the solar calendar, namely March 21 or March 22. The explanation for this is that *Nevruz* is associated with an earlier pre-Islamic holiday that celebrated the coming of spring.

9. Deborah Tannen (1984); Dennis Tedlock (1983); Allen Grimshaw (1982); Peter Trudgill (1986).

10. No particular event signaled the end of taping; instead a combination of circumstances together led to its demise. Among these circumstances is the greater amount of time that letter-writing takes during lessons. As Baba's eyesight has deteriorated, I have taken over Baba's correspondence. He dictates in whatever language and I write or translate. Another circumstance that contributed to the reduction of taping was my acceptance of Baba's inevitable death. In a way, by taping interaction with Baba I was trying to preserve what cannot be preserved. I still tape occasionally, but only infrequently.

11. In my early years of study with Baba, we tended to read aloud more. *Divans*, or collections of poems and nefes, that we read then include those of Yunus Emre (thirteenth-century Turkish) Omar Khayyam (fourteenth-century Persian), and Shah Ismail (sixteenth-century Persian) among others. Baba read then, too, as his eyesight was better. I have no recollection of the reason for the choice of the particular books. The only sure thing was that once we began, we always read through to the end of the book.

12. See Tannen (1984) for "times of misunderstanding"; Erickson (1979) for "uncomfortable moments."

13. It should be noted that Schegloff looked at many instances of short interactions (telephone conversations with emergency lines), and so my listing of him with the others may be misleading. Whereas Pittinger et al., Scollon, Labov and Fanshel, and Tannen all analyzed one interaction of the time frame given, Schegloff looked at many interactions, albeit much shorter ones.

14. I do not present Baba's interview by the professor to belittle the professor and thereby raise my standing. I had, at the time of the Hizir lesson, studied with Baba for twelve years. The interview was the professor's first contact with Baba. I chose to present the interview because I believe it influenced the Hizir lesson and because it provides an illuminating contrast with the lesson. In the rest of the book, it is my own confusions and ill-starred initiatives that I describe.

15. This sort of "oppression" of interviewee by interviewer is precisely what Charles Briggs refers to in his book *Learning How to Ask* (1986). See this book for a thorough discussion of problems of interview research, particularly in cross-

cultural contexts. Briggs not only presents the problems in both theory and practice, but also concerns himself with methodology to counteract or at least confront crucial ethnocentrism in interview research.

16. Attunement is a major theme of John Dewey's in his *Art as Experience* (1934).

17. Paul Ricoeur (1981), 182.

18. Hans-Georg Gadamer (1976), xxiii.

19. Humberto Maturana and Francisco Varela (1987), 75.

Chapter II: The Interactive Structure of Episodes in a Lesson

1. See Fiksdal (1986) for an especially good review of studies on interview.

2. See Sinclair and Coulthard (1975) and Brown and Yule (1983) for reviews of studies of teacher-student interaction.

3. Hedging is usually defined at the phrasal level, with such expressions as "sort of," "kind of," and so forth, which keep the speaker from committing herself or himself directly to a point. In the example from the lesson with Baba, however, I use hedging in the broader frame of "holding back from the point."

4. This is just a reminder to speakers of Turkish that Baba's spoken Turkish is a regional variety known as West Rumelian Turkish (see Appendix C). When Baba writes, however, he uses a Standard if archaic Turkish. In reading he prefers Turkish in the Ottoman script.

5. Goffman (1981) uses the term "back-channel cues," and Ochs (1983) refers to these affirmations as "response constants."

6. See Ochs, Schieffelin, and Platt (1978) for caretaker speech.

7. See again Briggs (1986) on problems of interview research in cross-cultural settings.

8. Dell Hymes has brought to my attention that parable-telling is not unitary. There are some parables whose meaning must be inferred by the hearer (like Baba's here), while there are other parables whose meaning is then explained by the teller (like some of Jesus' parables that he later explains to the disciples).

9. See page 000 for the story of the ant going on pilgrimage.

10. Schegloff, Jefferson, and Sacks (1977), 376.

11. The Michigan tekke is half an hour by car from the island south of Detroit where I grew up. As a child I was driven past the tekke many times. Although we never stopped there and I did not know what it was, its sign, "Albanian-American Teqe Bektashiane," must have registered in my mind.

12. On my first visit to the tekke, to my astonishment I heard Baba speaking Turkish. I did not know then that Turkish had been the main language of the Bektashis. I recognized the language because I had begun to study it the year before and was studying it then at the university. I visited the tekke several times before the other baba, Baba Bayram ("Bajram" in Albanian), invited me to study with Baba Rexheb.

13. Goffman (1981), 73.

Chapter III: Keying Interaction with Baba

1. The translation from the Arabic is mine. A. L. Becker also deserves credit for refusing to accept my earlier, murkier attempts.

The gender specific language reflects the Arabic original. When Baba quotes the poem in Turkish, however, it is no longer gender specific because Turkish has no distinction between "he" and "she." Both are *"o"* in Turkish. I wish I could have rendered the poem closer to the Turkish.

2. See Hymes (1983) in Bain, ed., 199–200, for a framework that brings together Brown and Levinson's (1987) "positive" and "negative politeness" with Goffman's (1967) earlier distinction of "deference" and "demeanor," and then expands the framework in a logical and illuminating manner.

3. Those familiar with Goffman's work will detect here an "attunement" to Goffman's language.

4. Much but not all research on conversation has confined itself to short exchanges. An example of research not so confined is Gail Jefferson's (1985) "On the Interactional Unpackaging of a Gloss."

My design in the present book was to present interaction beyond short exchanges but also of such character that readers would actually care about what was said. If I have succeeded in any way it is thanks to the value both traditional Islamic and Albanian cultures have placed on artistry in talk, a value that allowed for the cultivation of masters like Baba.

5. For speakers of Turkish, Baba's *uli* here (sometimes *olu*) is dialectal for the more standard *ölü*, "the dead one."

6. See my article on Albanian Muslims in America (1992) for a less cursory discussion of Baba's role in the Albanian community.

Chapter IV: Texture of Interaction with Baba

1. The question arises of how common a game is this building on each other's language. In terms of Baba's and my interaction it is most common, but in my first years of study with him it was of course less because we had fewer shared experiences. In terms of other talibs' experiences with Baba I do not have tapes to prove it, but my observation of Baba relating to other members of the tekke is that both Baba and they also build on each other's language and times together.

2. "Code-switching," or moving within the same conversation into another language, usually the native language of both participants, has been studied particularly in Hispanic contexts. With Baba and myself, however, our switching here involves moving from a third language (Turkish) into our differing native languages. Hymes graciously pointed out the unusualness of this sort of code-switching.

3. Morphophonemics is the intersection of word structure and sound structure of a language. In Turkish with its vowel harmony this is an interesting area. The simplest form of this harmony implies that in a Turkish word the vowels will

be either all front vowels (*gelmek, gitmek*) or all back vowels (*bakmak, vurmak*). When a suffix is added, and Turkish is very much a suffixing language, the vowels of the suffix will conform to the frontness or backness of the vowels of the word, resulting in: gelmek-te, gitmek-te, but bakmak-ta, vurmak-ta.

4. Verses 65 to 82 of Sura XVIII, the Sura of the Cave (quoted from N.J. Dawood's translation, *The Koran*, 1956):

> They went back by the way they came and found one of Our servants (Hizir) to whom We had vouchsafed Our mercy and whom We had endowed with knowledge of Our own. Moses said to him: "May I follow you so that you may guide me by that which you have been taught?"
>
> "You will not bear with me," replied the other. "For how can you bear with that which is beyond your knowledge?"
>
> Moses said: "If Allah wills, you shall find me patient; I shall not in anything disobey you."
>
> He said: "If you are bent on following me, you must ask no question about anything till I myself speak to you concerning it."
>
> The two set forth, but as soon as they embarked, Moses' companion bored a hole in the bottom of the ship.
>
> "A strange thing you have done!" exclaimed Moses. "Is it to drown her passengers that you have bored a hole in her?"
>
> "Did I not tell you," he replied, "that you would not bear with me?"
>
> "Pardon my forgetfulness," said Moses. "Do not be angry with me on account of this."
>
> They journeyed on until they fell in with a certain youth. Moses' companion slew him, and Moses said: "You have killed an innocent man who has done no harm. Surely you have committed a wicked crime."
>
> "Did I not tell you," he replied, "that you would not bear with me?"
>
> Moses said: "If ever I question you again, abondon me; for then I should deserve it."
>
> They travelled on until they came to a certain city. They asked the people for some food, but they declined to receive them as their guest. There they found a wall on the point of falling down. His companion restored it, and Moses said: "Had you wished, you could have demanded payment for your labours."
>
> "Now has the time arrived when we must part," said the other. "But first I will explain to you those acts of mine which you could not bear to watch with patience."
>
> "Know that the ship belonged to some poor fishermen. I damaged it because in their rear there was a king who was taking every ship by force.
>
> "As for the youth, his parents both are true believers, and we feared lest he should plague them with his wickedness and unbelief. It was our wish that their Lord should grant them another in his place, a son more righteous and more filial.
>
> "As for the wall, it belonged to two orphan boys in the city whose father was an honest man. Beneath it their treasure is buried. Your Lord decreed in

His mercy that they should dig out their treasure when they grew to manhood. What I did was not done by my will.

"That is the meaning of what you could not bear to watch with patience."

(Baba's tellings of the encounter of Musa and Hizir never include the second incident given above, in which the young man is killed.)

5. Ideally I would like to be able to compare the way Baba teaches me with the way he teaches other talibs. Unfortunately such teaching of others is difficult to observe systematically. The feature I have noticed most in his relationships with others is flexibility. He moves easily from a formal seriousness during prayers for specific requests to playful teasing to thoughtful regard and recall of people's concerns. Teenagers have also remarked to me how nonjudgmental he is, unlike their immigrant parents. I can only assume that Baba teaches in ways appropriate to each talib. I would assume that playful recollecting of shared talk would be an important part of this.

6. Bakhtin is certainly not the only theorist to note that a purpose of art is to offer closure; there is a rhetorical tradition in the United States, including scholars like Kenneth Burke, that also makes this point, and more recent literary critics such as Barbara Herrnstein Smith have also drawn together poetry and closure. The European vogue, to which my single listing of Bakhtin contributes, has often ignored those closer to home. I am indebted to Dell Hymes and A. L. Becker for calling this to my attention.

Chapter V: Bektashi Frame of Learning

1. *Muhiban* is the plural of *muhib*. A muhib is one who has gone through the private initiation ceremony of the Bektashi. For lay people, it is the last ritual step. For clericals, however, it is the first ritual step on the Bektashi ladder.

2. Fatimeh or Fatima is the daughter of the Prophet Muhammad. She married Ali, who is seen as the source of mystic knowledge in Islam. She is also the mother of Hasan and Husein, both of whom were killed. Hasan was poisoned and Husein was martyred on the field of battle at Kerbela. The main public holiday of the Bektashis as well as of Shi'a Muslims is commemoration of Husein's death, known as Ashura.

3. Baba Rexhebi (1970), 296.

4. "Oil-lamps" is a translation of the Albanian *kandile*. The murshid's reference to the young Ali Baba and his friend as oil-lamps is a prediction that they will become "lights" of the Bektashi Way for others.

5. Gazel or ghazal is the name in classical Arabic literature for a lyric poem. Many of the nefes belong to this category, although some that are of freer form are better classified as folk poetry.

6. Naim Frashëri (1846–1900) is the most famous poet of the Albanian national renaissance of the nineteenth century. He is also famous for being a

Bektashi. He looked to the religious tolerance of Bektashism as a model for the cooperation of Albanians who in a census conducted early in this century were 70 percent Muslim, 20 percent Eastern Orthodox, and 10 percent Roman Catholic.

7. Aşıks here refers to people who are drawn to a baba but who are not initiated members of a tekke.

8. A translation of this quatrain is found in the Introduction, but for convenient reference I repeat it here.

> I am Pir Sultan, so much you have let yourself fall.
>> Without greeting, you come and you pass by.
> Why do you flee this loving affection {touching muhabbet}?
>> Is this to be the emblem of our way?

Chapter VI: Learning as Attunement

1. An exception is Martin Lings' *A Sufi Saint of the Twentieth Century: Shaikh Ahmad al-Alawi* (1971), the first section of which is a description of a meeting with the Shaikh.

2. The most comprehensive biography of Helen Keller and Annie Sullivan is Joseph Lash's *Helen and Teacher* (1980).

3. Ann Hartman, formerly professor of Social Work at the University of Michigan, and currently Director of the Program in Social Work at Smith College, first suggested the parallel of Annie Sullivan and Helen Keller to the relationship of murshid and talib during an extended discussion of that relationship. I am most grateful to her for this and other counsel.

4. Bambi Schieffelin (1981), 189–196.

5. Again the question arises, How typical is my experience as talib with Baba? Do other talibs meet as often? Some talibs are at the tekke frequently, serving Baba in various ways and being with him. There are talibs, however, who are rarely there, especially those who live outside the Detroit area in Chicago, Connecticut, New Jersey, or even Australia. The ones in America but outside Michigan come at least once or more a year, and often they stay at the tekke for several days or several weeks. Those from other continents cannot do this, yet their very request for initiation I see as a way of being spiritually closer to Baba when they cannot be geographically close. Each of these people must, however, find an already initiated sponsor for initiation. As might be expected, their preparation time is limited by practical considerations.

6. Of course Baba had earlier spoken to me through nefes, but it had seemed more elaborative than central. In the basement kitchen scene, however, the nefes was the vehicle through which I finally grasped muhabbet and realized how nefes could be a central vehicle for communication.

7. I have translated the Turkish *insan* here as "a man," for reasons of verbal stress and not to imply any gender exclusion. "Insan" better translates as "human being." Unfortunately, "human" has the verbal stress on the wrong syllable for the line. Note, however, that all references to the line refer to "human"—a relatively gender-free designation.

Appendix A: Conventions of Transcription

FT   my initials signifying my speech

..   a pause of one second (each dot signifies a half-second pause)

\   geldi\
     falling intonation at end of word

~   amerikada~
     signifies high pitch, especially common in Turkish;
     suggests speaker is not finished

?   yes/no question, rising intonation

-      bu-
     signifies cutting off of sound, as in a false start

CAPITAL letters of a word or SYLlable
     indicate emphatic stress
         (Note that here, unlike the case for most other studies of
         conversation, I have retained capitalization for proper
         nouns for easier reading; BaBA implies that there is em-
         phasis on last syllable only.)

< >   \<ehl-i tarik >
     signifies set-off phrase, special sort of emphasis;
     Baba sometimes uses when he quotes non-Turkish phrases

{ }   {softly}, {Arabic}
     states sort of change from preceding talk;
     for example, in tone of voice or in language

\ \   \amerikada\
     signifies that phrase reflects intonation pattern of immediately
     preceding phrase

-      -murshid
     at start of line, signifies that it is a continuation of preceding
     line without significant pause or change in intonation

spacing of start of next turn
              below the end of the previous one
          signifies that there was no perceptible pause between turns

[placed one above the other show   [initial place
                                              [of overlap of talk

bold within a transcript of dialogue
          highlights point to be addressed
          in surrounding discussion

RELATING TO TURKISH AND ALBANIAN
The Turkish alphabet has six symbols not found in the English alphabet:

ç ("ch")
ş ("sh")
ü (front high rounded vowel)
ö (front central rounded vowel)
ğ (lengthens previous vowel)
ı (signifies an undotted "i"
     high, central, unrounded vowel)

The Albanian alphabet has nine symbols and letter combinations not found in English:

ç   ("ch")
dh   ("th" as in "they")
ë   ("uh," central unrounded vowel)
gj   ("g + y")
ll   (back "l")
nj   ("n + y")
rr   (strong flap)
xh   ("j" as in "job")
zh   (as in French "je")

Appendix B: Turkish Texts of Nefes

Where Baba's version differs from the printed version in Sadeddin Nuzhet Ergün's *Bektashi Şairleri ve Nefesleri* (1960), Baba's words are added in parentheses.

In recitation, Baba often repeats each line of the third quatrain, chanting "hu" after each repetition. He also adds "hu" at the end of most stanzas and invariably at the end of the whole nefes.

by Pir Sultan Abdal (sixteenth century)

> Derdim çoktur kangisına yanayim
>   Yine tazelendi yürek yaresi
> Ben bu derde kande derman bulayim
>   Meğer Şah elinden ola çaresi

> Türlü donlar giyer gülden naziktir
>   Bülbül cevr eyleme güle yazıktır
> Çok hasretlik çektim bağrım eziktir
>   Güle güle gelir canlar paresi

> Benim uzun boylu servi cinarım
>   Yüreğime bir od düştü yanarım
> Kiblem sensin yüzüm sana dönerim
>   Mihrabımdır kaşlarının (iki kaşın) arası

> Didar ile mahabbete (mahabbet'le) doyulmaz
>   Mahabbetten kaçan insan sayılmaz
> Münkir üflemekle çirag söyünmez
>   Tutuşunca yanar aşkın çirası

> Pir Sultan'ım kati (kani) yüksek uçarsın
>   Selamsız sabahsız gelir geçersin

Dilber (Güzel) mahabbetten niçin kaçarsın
Böyle midir yolumuzun turası

by Mehmet Ali Hilmi Dede Baba (nineteenth century)

Ayine tuttum yüzüme
Ali göründü gözüme
Nazar eyledim özüme
Ali göründü gözüme

Adem Baba Havva ile
Hem Alem el'esma ile
Çerhi felek sema ile
Ali göründü gözüme

Hazreti Nuh Neciyyullah
Hem Ibrahim Halilullah
Sinadaki Kelimullah
Ali göründü gözüme

Isayı Ruhullah oldur
Iki alemde Şah oldur
Mu'minlere penah oldur
Ali göründü gözüme

Ali evvel Ali ahir
Ali batın Ali zahir
Ali tayyib Ali tahir
Ali göründü gözüme

Ali candır Ali canan
Ali dindir Ali iman
Ali rahim Ali rahman
Ali göründü gözüme

Hilmi gedayi bir kemter
Görür gözüm dilim söyler
Her nereye kılsam nazar
Ali göründü gözüme

by Niyazi Mısri

Derman arardım derdime
    derdim bana derman imiş
Burhan aradım aslıma
    aslım bana burhan imiş

Sağ u solum gözler idim
    dost yüzünü görsem deyu
Ben tasrada arar idim
    ol can içinde can imiş

Öyle sanırdım ayriyem
    dost gayridir ben gayriyem
Benden görüp işiteni
    bildim ki ol canan imiş

Savm-i salat u hac ile
    sanma biter zahid işin
Insani-i kâmil olmağa
    lazim olan irfan imiş

Kande gelir yolun senin
    ya kande varır menzilin
Nerden gelüp gittiğini
    anlamayan hayvan imiş

Murşid gerektir bildire
    Hakk'i sana Hakk el-yakın
Murşidi olmayanların
    bildikleri guman imiş

Her murşide dil verme kim
    yolunu sarpa uğradır
Murşidi kâmil olanın
    gayet yolu asan imiş

Anla hemen bir sözdürür
    yokuş değildir düzdürür

Alem kamu bir yüzdürür
    gören ani hayran imiş

Işit Niyazi'nın sözün
    bir nesne örtmez Hak yüzün
Haktan ayan bir nesne yok
    gözsüzlere pinhan imiş

Appendix C: Features of West Rumelian Turkish, Baba's Dialect

"Rumelian Turkish" refers to the Turkish spoken in the Balkans. (The name "Rumeli" comes from the term the Ottoman Empire used to refer to its European provinces there.) As cited in *Philologiae Turcicae Fundamenta* (1959), the Turkish of the Balkans is further classified into East Rumelian Turkish and West Rumelian Turkish. Geographically, East Rumelian Turkish is spoken in most of Bulgaria, while West Rumelian Turkish is or was spoken in the far west of Bulgaria, in Yugoslavia, and in Albania.

This classification is largely based on the work of J. Nemeth, the eminent Hungarian Turcologist, in his monograph *Zur Einteiling der Türkischen Mundarten Bulgariens*, "On the Classification or Division of Turkish Dialects in Bulgaria," (Sofia, 1956). The monograph is much broader than its title would indicate. Nemeth includes data from regions beyond the borders of Bulgaria and relates differences in dialect to different times and places of origin of Turkish settlers in the Balkans.

In particular, Nemeth proposes eight distinctive isoglosses of West Rumelian Turkish. The first five of these isoglosses relate to a "breakdown" of vowel harmony—that progressive assimilation for which Standard Turkish is so famous—in which the first vowel in a word can be see as keying the following vowels of that word in terms of frontness (*öldü*) and unroundedness (*baktı*).

West Rumelian Turkish: Nemeth's Eight Isoglosses

with contrasting examples of Standard form and dialect form

1. ı, u, ü → i in word final position.
   (öldü—oldi)
2. the perfect suffix -miş is invariant.
   (kalkmış—kalkmiş)

3. i → ı in noninitial and closed final syllables.
(benim—benım)
4. ö → o', o; and ü → u' in many words.
(dört—dort; üç—uç)
5. in suffixes with low vowel harmony (e ~ a), one of the two forms is
generalized.
(kanlar—kanler)
6. ö → ü in about forty words.
(ördek—ürdek)
7. Osmanli ğ is preserved as g.
(ağaç—agaç)
8. the progressive participle form in -yor is replaced by one in -y.
(seviyorum—seveyi-m)

In a later article by Nemeth, "Traces of the Turkish Language in Albania" (1961), an article that was most generously brought to my attention by Professor Victor Friedman, Nemeth proposes two additional isoglosses for the Turkish of Albania:

9. fronting of k and g to palatal affricates or stops.
(gyun or djun for gün, kyi for ki)
10. variations in word-initial h.

The first of these additional isoglosses (9) is not a feature of Baba's Turkish in voiced form (gü → gyu) but is present in unvoiced form (ki →kyı). In my recent travels in Yugoslavia (1987 to 1988) I noted both of these as most prominent in the Turkish spoken in Kossovo and western Macedonia, and in the Albanian of those regions.

Nemeth does not systematically discuss morphology and syntax of West Rumelian Turkish in his articles. These are discussed, however, in a study by Victor Friedman, "Balkanology and Turcology: West Rumelian Turkish in Yugoslavia as Reflected in Prescriptive Grammar" (1982: 13–25, 30–31).

Selected Features of Morphology and Syntax from Friedman's Study on West Rumelian Turkish

The following features are represented in Baba's Turkish.

Morphology

1. invariant -miş
2. participle + auxiliary (separation of idi, e.g. var idi)
3. datives (generalization of -a or -e no matter the frontness or backness
      of vowel)
4. verbal derivations, especially with -len- or -lan-

Syntax

1. placement of verb in nonfinal position (exceedingly common)
2. use of optative-subjunctive in place of other finite and nonfinite verbal
      forms as calques in Albanian subordinite clauses in të

   Besides these published dialect features, the following four are additional features of Baba's Turkish that I find interesting and that are probably dialectal. (Indeed, Baba's Turkish deserves a study of its own.)

Additional Selected Features of Baba's Dialect

1. nominal use of bu referring to a person
      (Bu geldi, i.e., Bu adam geldi, similar to Albanian usage
      of ky and kjo)
2. reduction or inversion in the genitive construction
      (onun arkadaşı ismi Mustafa)
3. use of locative suffix instead of dative
      (giderlerdi tekkede)
4. peculiarities of postpredicate elements

   In reference to number 3 above, the only place I find published reference to this phenomenon is in Tadeusz Kowalski's *Les Turcs et la langue
Turque de la Bulgarie du Nord-Est* (1933)—a study on what would now be
considered an East Rumelian Turkish. And in reference to the last feature
listed above, number 4, I find interesting differences between the findings
of Dan Slobin and Karl Zimmer's study (1986) on postpredicate elements
in spoken Turkish and Baba's speech (recall that their study was with Standard speakers of Turkish).

Baba has a higher percentage of postpredicate elements that are objects (80 percent) than was found in Slobin and Zimmer's study, but only half the percentage of subjects in that position that the researchers found. Further, in Baba's narratives, the percentage of postpredicate elements increases from a low of 25 percent to a high of 66 percent when going from narratives of little action to passages of dramatic action. There is clearly a discourse constraint on this feature.

Bibliography

Abd-Allah, Umar. "The Phenomenon of Language in the Qur'an." Unpublished paper, Near Eastern Studies, University of Michigan, 1980.

Abul Quasem, Muhammad. *The Recitation and Interpretation of the Qur'an: Al-Ghazali's Theory.* Kuala Lumpur: University of Malaya Press, 1979.

Abu-Lughod, Lila. *Veiled Sentiments: Honor and Poetry in a Bedouin Society.* Berkeley: University of California Press, 1986.

Allen, Harold B. and Michael D. Linn, eds. *Dialect and Language Variation.* New York: Academic Press, 1986.

Anderson, Anne, Gillian Brown, Gordon Shillcock, and George Yule. *Teaching Talk: Strategies for Production and Assessment.* Cambridge: Cambridge University Press, 1984.

Andrews, Walter. *An Introduction to Ottoman Poetry.* Minneapolis, Minn.: Bibliotheca Islamica, 1976.

———. *Poetry's Voice, Society's Song: Ottoman Lyric Poetry.* Seattle: University of Washington Press, 1985.

Antoun, Richard. *Muslim Preacher in the Modern World: A Jordanian Case Study in Comparative Perspective.* Princeton, N.J.: Princeton University Press, 1989.

Ayoub, Mahmoud M. *The Qur'an and Its Interpreters.* Vol. 1. Albany: State University of New York Press, 1984.

Babcock, Barbara. "The Story in the Story: Meta-Narration in Folk Narrative." In Richard Bauman, ed., *Verbal Art as Performance.* Rowley, Mass.: Newbury House, 1977, 61–79.

Basso, Ellen. *A Musical View of the Universe:* Philadelphia: University of Pennsylvania Press, 1985.

Bateson, Gregory. *Steps to an Ecology of Mind.* New York: Ballantine, 1972.

Bauman, Richard. *Let Your Words Be Few: Symbolism of Speaking and Silence Among Seventeenth-Century Quakers.* Cambridge: Cambridge University Press, 1983.

———, ed. *Verbal Art as Performance.* Rowley, Mass.: Newbury House, 1977.

de Beaugrande, Robert. "Text and Discourse in European Research." *Discourse Processes* 3 (1980), 287–300.

Becker, Alton L. "Biography of a Sentence: A Burmese Proverb." In Edward M. Bruner, ed., *Text, Play, and Story: The Construction and Reconstruction of Self and Society.* Washington, D.C.: American Ethnological Society, 1984, 135—155.

———. "Beyond Translation: Esthetics and Language Description." In Heidi Byrnes ed., *Contemporary Perceptions of Language: Interdisciplinary Dimensions.* Georgetown Roundtable on Language and Linguistics. Washington, D.C.: Georgetown University Press, 1982 , 124–138.

———. "Epistemology and Aesthetics in Javanese Shadow Theatre." In A. L.

Becker and Aram Yengoyan eds., *The Imagination of Reality: Essays in South-east Asian Coherence Systems*. Norwood, N.J.: Ablex, 1979.

———. "The Figure a Sentence Makes: An Interpretation of a Classical Malay Sentence." In Talmy Givón, ed., *Discourse and Syntax*. Syntax and Semantics, vol. 12. New York: Academic Press, 1979, 243–259.

———. "Philology and Logophilia: An Exploratory Essay." Henry Hoijer Lecture, University of Southern California at Los Angeles, 1984.

Beeman, William O. *Language, Status, and Power in Iran*. Bloomington: Indiana University Press, 1986.

Bennett, Adrian. "Interruptions and the Interpretation of Conversation." *Discourse Processes* 4 (1981), 171–88.

Benveniste, Émile, Noam Chomsky, Roman Jakobson, and André Martinet. *Problèmes du langage*. Paris: Gallimard, 1966.

———. *Problems in General Linguistics*. Trans. Mary Elizabeth Meek. Coral Gables, Fla.: University of Miami Press, 1971.

Birge, John Kingsley. *The Bektashi Order of Dervishes*. London: Luzac & Co., 1937.

Black Elk. *Black Elk Speaks: Being the Life Story of a Holy Man of the Oglala Sioux*. As told through John G. Neihardt. New York: Washington Square Press, 1959; reprint Pocket Books, 1972.

Bloch, Maurice, ed. *Political Language and Oratory in Traditional Society*. New York: Academic Press, 1975.

Bloom, Harold. *The Anxiety of Influence: A Theory of Poetry*. Oxford: Oxford University Press, 1973.

Blum, David. *The Art of Quartet Playing: The Guarneri Quartet in Conversation with David Blum*. New York: Knopf, 1986.

Brazil, David. "Intonation and Discourse: Some Principles and Procedures." *Text* 3, 1 (1983), 39–70.

Briggs, Charles L. *Learning How to Ask: A Sociolinguistic Appraisal of the Role of the Interview in Social Science Research*. Cambridge: Cambridge University Press, 1986.

Brower, Reuben. *Mirror on Mirror: Translation, Imitation, Parody*. Cambridge, Mass.: Harvard University Press, 1974.

Brown, Gillian and George Yule. *Discourse Analysis*. Cambridge Textbooks in Linguistics. London: Cambridge University Press, 1983.

Brown, Penelope and Stephen Levinson. *Politeness: Some Universals in Language Usage*. Cambridge: Cambridge University Press, 1987.

Bruner, Jerome. *Child's Talk: Learning to Use Language*. New York: W. W. Norton, 1983.

Burke, Kenneth. "Literature as Equipment for Living." In Stanley Edgar Hyman, ed., *Perspectives in Incongruity*. Bloomington: Indiana University Press, 1937, 100–109.

———. *The Rhetoric of Religion: Studies in Logology*. Boston: Beacon Press, 1961; reprint, Berkeley: University of California Press, 1970.

Burton, Deirdre. *Dialogue and Discourse: A Sociolinguistic Approach to Modern Drama, Dialogue and Naturally Occurring Conversation*. London: Routledge & Kegan Paul, 1980.

Caton, Steven C. "Power, Persuasion, and Language." *International Journal of Middle East Studies* 19, 1 (1987), 77–102.

Chafe, Wallace. "The Flow of Thought and the Flow of Language." In Talmy Givon, ed., *Discourse and Syntax*. Syntax and Semantics, vol 12. New York: Academic Press, 1979, 159–81.

Chelkowski, Peter ed. *Ta'ziyet: Ritual and Drama in Iran*. New York: New York University Press, 1979.

Chittick, William. "The Words of the All-Merciful." *Parabola* 8, 3 (August 1983), 19–25.

Cicourel, Aaron V. "Three Models of Discourse Analysis: The Role of Social Structure." *Discourse Processes* 3 (1980), 101–31.

Clements, George N. and Engin Sezer. "Vowel and Consonant Disharmony in Turkish." In Harry van der Hulst and Norval Smith, eds., *The Structure of Phonological Representations* (part III). Dordrecht: Foris Publications, 1982, 213–55.

Corbin, Henry. *Creative Imagination in the Sufism of Ibn al-Arabi*. Trans. Ralph Manheim. Princeton, N.J.: Princeton University Press, 1969.

Corsaro, William A. "Communicative Processes in Studies of Social Organization: Sociological Approaches to Discourse Analysis." *Text* (1983), 5–63.

Coulthard, Malcolm. *An Introduction to Discourse Analysis*. Hong Kong: Longman, 1977.

Cruise O'Brien, Donal. *The Mourides of Senegal: The Political and Economic Organization of an Islamic Brotherhood*. Oxford: Clarendon Press, 1971.

Dawood, N. J. *The Koran*. Baltimore: Penguin, 1956. Third rev. ed. 1971.

Deny, Jean. *Grammaire de la langue turque (dialecte osmanli)*. Paris: Impriméerie Nationale, 1921.

Dewey, John. *Art as Experience*. New York: Minton Balch, 1934.

Ducrot, Oswald. *Dire et ne pas dire: principes de semantique linguistique*. Paris: Hermann, 1980.

Dundes, Alan, Jerry Leach, and Bora Özkök. "The Strategy of Turkish Boys' Verbal Dueling Rhymes." In John Gumperz and Dell Hymes, eds., *Directions in Sociolinguistics: The Ethnography of Communication*. New York: Holt, Rinehart & Winston, 1972, 130–40.

Dwyer, Kevin. *Moroccan Dialogues: Anthropology in Question*. Baltimore: Johns Hopkins University Press, 1982.

Erguvanli, Eser. "The Function of Word Order in Turkish Grammar." Unpublished Ph.D. dissertation, University of California at Los Angeles, 1979.

Erickson, Frederick. "Talking Down: Some Cultural Sources of Miscommunication in Interracial Interviews." In Aaron Wolfgang, ed., *Nonverbal Behavior: Aplications and Cultural Implications*. New York: Academic Press, 1979, 99–126.

Erickson, Frederick and Jeffrey Shultz. *The Counselor as Gatekeeper: Social Interaction in Interviews*. New York: Academic Press, 1982.

Feinberg, Harriet Adele. "Teacher and Student in Buber's Hasidic Tales." Unpublished Ph.D. dissertation, Department of Education, Harvard University, 1972.

Feld, Steven. *Sound and Sentiment: Birds, Weeping, Poetics, and Song in Kaluli Expression.* Philadelphia: University of Pennsylvania Press, 1982. Second ed., 1990.

Fernandez, James. "The Mission of Metaphor in Expressive Culture." *Current Anthropology* 15, 2 (June 1974), 119–43.

Fiksdal, Susan. "The Right Time and Pace." Unpublished Ph.D. dissertation, Linguistics Department, University of Michigan, 1986.

Fischer, Michael M. J. *Iran: From Religious Dispute to Revolution.* Cambridge, Mass.: Harvard University Press, 1980.

Fischer, Michael M. J. and Mehdi Abedi. *Debating Muslims: Cultural Dialogues in Postmodernity and Tradition.* Madison: University of Wisconsin Press, 1990.

Fisher, Sue. "Institutional Authority and the Structure of Discourse." *Discourse Processes* 7 (1984), 201–23.

Frankel, Richard M. "From Sentence to Sequence: Understanding the Medical Encounter Through Micro-Interactional Analysis." *Discourse Processes* 7 (1984), 135–70.

Friedman, Victor A. "Balkanology and Turcology: West Rumelian Turkish in Yugoslavia as Reflected in Prescriptive Grammar." *Studies in Slavic and General Linguistics* 4, 2 (1982), 40–77. Amsterdam: Rodopi.

Gadamer, Hans-Georg. *Philosophical Hermeneutics.* Trans. and ed. David E. Linge. Berkeley: University of California Press, 1976.

Geertz, Clifford. *Islam Observed: Religious Development in Morocco and Indonesia.* Chicago: University of Chicago Press, 1968.

———. *Local Knowledge: Further Essays in Interpretative Anthropology.* New York: Basic Books, 1983.

Gibb, E. J. W. *A History of Ottoman Poetry.* Vol. II (1902), vol III (1904). London: Luzac & Co.

Giglioli, Pier Paolo, ed. *Language and Social Context: Selected Readings.* New York: Penguin, 1972.

Giles, Howard, D. Taylor, and R. Bourhis. "Toward a Theory of Interpersonal Accommodation Through Speech: Some Canadian Details." *Language in Society* 2 (1973), 177—92.

Giles, Howard and P. Smith. "Accommodation Theory: Optimal Levels of Convergence." In Howard Giles and Robert N. St. Clair, eds., *Language and Social Psychology.* Oxford: Basil Blackwell, 1979.

Gilsenan, Michael. *Saint and Sufi in Modern Egypt: An Essay in the Sociology of Religion.* Oxford: Clarendon Press, 1973.

Givón, Talmy, ed. *Topic Continuity in Discourse: A Quantitative Cross-Language Study.* Typological Studies in Language, vol. 3. Amsterdam: J. Benjamins, 1983.

Goffman, Erving. *The Presentation of Self in Everyday Life.* Garden City, N.Y.: Doubleday, 1959.

———. *Encounters: Two Studies in the Sociology of Interaction.* Indianapolis: Bobbs-Merrill, 1961.

———. *Interaction Ritual: Essays on Face-to-Face Behavior.* New York: Doubleday, 1967.

————. *Frame Analysis*. New York: Harper and Row, 1974.

————. *Forms of Talk: An Essay on the Organization of Experience*. Philadelphia: University of Pennsylvania Press, 1981.

Goody, Esther N. "Towards a Theory of Questions." In Esther N. Goody, ed., *Questions and Politeness: Strategies in Social Interaction*. Cambridge Papers in Social Anthropology no. 8. Cambridge: Cambridge University Press, 1978, 17–43.

Graham, William A. *Beyond the Written Word: Oral Aspects of Scripture in the History of Religion*. Cambridge: Cambridge University Press, 1987.

Green, Arthur. *Tormented Master: A Life of Rabbi Nahman of Bratslav*. University: University of Alabama Press, 1979.

Greenberg, Joseph. "Universals of Kinship Terminology: Their Names and the Problem of Their Explanation." In Jacques Maquet, ed., *On Linguistic Anthropology: Essays in Honor of Harry Hoijer*. Malibu, Calif.: Undena Publications, 1980.

Grimshaw, Allen. "Comprehensive Discourse Analysis: An Instance of Professional Peer Interaction." *Language in Society* 11, 1 (April 1982), 15–47.

Gumperz, John J. *Discourse Strategies*. Cambridge: Cambridge University Press, 1982.

Halliday, M. A. K. and Ruqaiya Hasan. *Cohesion in English*. Bath: Pitman Press, 1976.

Harris, Roy. *The Language-Makers*. Ithaca, N.Y.: Cornell University Press, 1980.

Hawkes, Terence. *Structuralism and Semiotics*. Berkeley: University of California Press, 1977.

Herrigel, Eugen. *Zen in the Art of Archery*. New York: Vintage Books, 1971.

Heyd, Uriel. *Language Reform in Modern Turkey*. Jerusalem: Israel Oriental Society, 1954.

Hiz, Henry, ed. *Questions*. Dordrecht: D. Reidel, 1978.

Hopper, Paul. "Aspect and Foregrounding in Discourse." In Talmy Givón, ed., *Discourse and Syntax*. Syntax and Semantics, vol. 12. New York: Academic Press, 1979.

Hoy, David Couzens. *The Critical Circle*. Berkeley: University of California Press, 1982.

Hudson, R. A. *Sociolinguistics*. Cambridge Textbooks in Linguistics. London: Cambridge University Press, 1980.

Hymes, Dell. "Models of the Interaction of Language and Social Life." in John Gumperz, and Dell Hymes, eds., *Directions in Sociolinguistics: The Ethnography of Communication*. New York: Holt, Rinehart & Winston, 1972, 35–71.

————. *Foundations in Sociolinguistics*. Philadelphia: University of Pennsylvania Press, 1974.

————. *"In vain I tried to tell you": Essays in Native American Ethnopoetics*. Philadelphia: University of Pennsylvania Press, 1981.

————. "Report from an Underdeveloped Country: Toward Linguistic Competence in the United States." In Bruce Bain, ed., *The Sociogenesis of Language and Human Conduct*. New York: Plenum Press, 1983, 189–224.

Keeney, Bradford P. *Aesthetics of Change*. New York: Guilford Press, 1983.

Jakobson, Roman. "Concluding Statement: Linguistics and Poetics." In Thomas A. Sebeok, ed., *Style in Language*. Cambridge, Mass.: MIT Press, 1960.

———. *The Framework of Language*. Michigan Studies in the Humanities, vol. 1. Ann Arbor: Rackham School of Graduate Studies, University of Michigan, 1980.

———. *Verbal Art, Verbal Sign, Verbal Time*. Minneapolis: University of Minnesota Press, 1985. Based on a special issue of *Poetics Today* (autumn 1980).

Jefferson, Gail. "Side Sequences." In David Sudnow, ed., *Studies in Social Interaction*. New York: Free Press, 1972, 294–338.

———. "On the Interactional Unpacking of a Gloss." *Language in Society* 4, 14 (1985), 435–66.

Karaosmanoğlu, Yakup Kadri. *Nur Baba*. Istanbul: Remzi Kitabevi, 1948.

Kowalski, Tadeusz. *Les Turcs et la langue Turque de la Bulgarie du Nord-Est*. Paris: Librairie Franco-Polanaise et Étrangère, 1933.

Labov, William. *Sociolinguistic Patterns*. Philadelphia: University of Pennsylvania Press, 1972.

Labov, William and David Fanshel. *Therapeutic Discourse: Psychotherapy as Conversation*. New York: Academic Press, 1977.

Lakoff, Robin. "Language in Context." *Language* 48 (1972), 907–27.

Lash, Joseph. *Helen and Teacher: The Story of Helen Keller and Anne Sullivan Macy*. New York: Delacorte Press, 1980.

Lees, Robert B. *The Phonology of Modern Standard Turkish*. Bloomington: Indiana University Publications, 1961.

Levinson, Stephen C. "Some Pre-Observations on the Modelling of Dialogue." *Discourse Processes* 4 (1981), 93–116.

———. *Pragmatics*. Cambridge: Cambridge University Press, 1983.

Lewis, Geoffrey. *Turkish Grammar*. Oxford: Clarendon Press, 1967.

Lings, Martin. *A Sufi Saint of the Twentieth Century: Shaikh Ahmad al-Alawi*. London: Allen & Unwin, 1971.

———. *What is Sufism?* Berkeley: University of California Press, 1975.

Malamud, Susan. "The Master-Disciple Relationship in Eleventh- Century Khurasan." Unpublished paper from the Middle East Studies Association Annual Meeting, San Antonio, Texas, 1980.

Mannheim, Bruce. "Couplets and Oblique Contexts: The Social Organization of a Folksong." *Text* VII (1987), 265–88.

Maturana, Humberto and Francisco Varela. *Autopoiesis and Cognition: The Realization of the Living*. Dordrecht: D. Reidel, 1980.

———. *The Tree of Knowledge: The Biological Roots of Human Understanding*. Boston: Shambhala Publications, New Science Library, 1987.

Mauriac, Claude. *Le dîner en ville. The Dinner Party*. Trans. Merloyd Lawrence. New York: Delta, 1963.

McTear, Michael. *Children's Conversation*. London: Basil Blackwell, 1985.

Michalowski, Piotr. "Carminative Magic: Towards an Understanding of Sumerian Poetics." In W. von Soden, ed., *Zeitschrift für Assyriologie und Vorderasiatissche Archäologie*. Berlin: Walter de Gruyter, 1981.

Muggeridge, Malcolm. *Something Beautiful for God: Mother Teresa of Calcutta*. Garden City, N.Y.: Image Books, 1971.

Mundy, C. S. "Turkish Syntax as a System of Qualification." *British School of Oriental and African Studies* XVII, 12 (1955), 279–305.

Myers, Terry, ed. *The Development of Conversation and Discourse*. Edinburgh: Edinburgh University Press, 1979.

Nash, Rose. *Turkish Intonation: An Instrumental Study*. The Hague: Mouton, 1973.

Nemeth, J. *Zur Einteilung der Türkischen Mundarten Bulgariens*. Sofia: Bulgarische Akademie der Wissenschaften, 1956.

———. "Traces of the Turkish Language in Albania." *Acta Orientalia Hungarica* 13 (1961), 8–29.

Newmark, Leonard, and Philip Hubbard, and Peter Prifti. *Standard Albanian: A Reference Grammar for Students*. Stanford, Calif.: Stanford University Press, 1982.

Ochs, Elinor and Bambi B. Schieffelin. *Acquiring Conversational Competence*. London: Routledge & Kegan Paul, 1983.

———. *Developmental Pragmatics*. New York: Academic Press, 1979.

Ochs, Elinor, Bambi Schieffelin, and M. Platt. "Questions of Immediate Concern." In E. N. Goody, ed., *Questions and Politeness: Strategies in Social Interaction*. Cambridge: Cambridge University Press, 1978.

Pellegrini, Anthony and Thomas Yawkey, eds. *The Development of Oral and Written Language in Social Contexts*. In Roy Freedle, ed., Advances in Discourse Processes, vol. XIII. Norwood, N.J.: Ablex, 1984.

Pickthall, Mohammad Marmaduke. *The Meaning of the Glorious Koran: An Explanatory Translation*. 1930. New York: Mentor, 1985.

Pipa, Arshi. "Albanian Folk Verse: Structure and Genre." In *Albanische Forschungen* 17. Munich: Dr. Rudolf Trofenik, 1978.

Pittenger, R. E., Charles Hockett, and J. J. Danehy. *The First Five Minutes*. Ithaca N.Y.: Paul Martineau, 1960.

Rappaport, Roy A. *Ecology, Meaning, and Religion*. Richmond, Calif.: North Atlantic Books, 1979.

Redhouse, J. W. "'The Most Comely Names,' i.e. the laudatory epithets, or the titles of praise bestowed on God in the Qur'an or by Muslim Writers." Royal Asiatic Society of Great Britain and Ireland (January 1880). In Pamphlets of Sir J. W. Redhouse.

———. *A Simplified Grammar of the Ottoman-Turkish Language*. London: Trubner, 1884.

———. *A Turkish and English Lexicon*. Constantinople: Boyajian, 1890.

Rexhebi, Baba. *Misticizma Islame dhe Bektshizma*. New York: Waldon Press, 1970.

Richmond, Mary E. *What Is Social Care Work?* New York: Russell Sage, 1922.

Ricoeur, Paul. *Hermeneutics and the Human Sciences: Essays on Language, Action, and Interpretation*. Ed. and trans. John B. Thompson. Cambridge: Cambridge University Press, 1981.

Rueckert, William H. *Kenneth Burke and the Drama of Human Relations*. Berkeley: University of California Press, 1982.

Ruesch, Jurgen and Gregory Bateson. *Communication: The Social Matrix of Psychiatry*. New York: W. W. Norton, 1951.

Rypka, Jan. *History of Iranian Literature*. Dordrecht: D. Reidel, 1968.

Sacks, Harvey, Emanuel Schegloff, and Gail Jefferson. "A Simplest Systematics for the Organization of Turn Taking for Conversation." *Language* 50, 4 (1974), 696–735.

Said, Edward W. *Orientalism*. New York: Pantheon Books, 1978.

Schachter, Zalman Meshull. "The Encounter (Yehidut): A Study of Counselling in Hasidism." Unpublished Ph.D. dissertation, Hebrew Union College, 1968.

Schegloff, Emanuel. "The First Five Seconds: The Order of Conversational Openings." PhD. dissertation, University of California, Berkeley, 1967.

———. "Sequencing in Conversational Openings." *American Anthropologist* 70, 4 (1968), 1075–95.

———. "Notes on a Conversational Practice: Formulating Place." In David Sudnow, ed., *Studies in Social Interaction*. New York: Free Press, 1972.

Schegloff, Emanuel and Harvey Sacks. "Opening up Closings," *Semiotica* VIII, 4 (1973), 289–327.

Schegloff, Emanuel, Gail Jefferson, and Harvey Sacks. "The Preference for Self-Correction in the Organization of Repair in Conversation." *Language* 53 (1977), 361–82.

Schenkein, Jim, ed. *Studies in the Organization of Conversational Interaction*. New York: Academic Press, 1978.

Schieffelin, Bambi B. "A Sociolinguistic Analysis of a Relationship." *Discourse Processes* 4 (1981), 189–96.

Schimmel, Annemarie. *And Muhammad Is His Messenger: The Veneration of the Prophet in Islamic Piety*. Chapel Hill: University of North Carolina Press, 1985.

Scollon, Ronald. *Conversations with a One Year Old: A Case Study of the Developmental Foundation of Syntax*. Honolulu: University of Hawaii Press, 1976.

Scollon, Ronald and Suzanne Scollon. *Linguistic Convergence: An Ethnography of Speaking at Fort Chipewyan, Alberta*. New York: Academic Press, 1979.

Sebüktekin, Hikmet. *Turkish-English Contrastive Analysis*. The Hague: Mouton, 1970.

Shah, Idries. *Learning How to Learn*. London: Octagon Press, 1978.

Sherzer, Joel. "Tellings, Retellings, and Tellings Within Tellings: the Structuring and Organization of Narrative in Kuna Indian Discourse." Sociolinguistic Working Paper no. 83, Southwest Educational Development Laboratory, 1981, 1–24.

Sinclair, John McH. and Malcolm Coulthard. *Towards an Analysis of Discourse: The English Used by Teachers and Pupils*. London: Oxford University Press, 1975.

Silverstein, Michael. "The Culture of Language in Chinookan Narrative Texts; or, On saying that . . . in Chinook." In Johanna Nicholls and Anthony C. Woodbury, eds., *Grammar Inside and Outside the Clause*. Cambridge: Cambridge University Press, 1985, 132–71.

Slobin, Dan I. and Karl Zimmer. *Studies in Turkish Linguistics*. Typological Studies in Language, vol. 8. Philadelphia: John Benjamins, 1986.

Stern, Daniel. *The First Relationship: Mother and Infant*. Cambridge, Mass.: Harvard University Press, 1977.

Stewart, Susan. "Shouts on the Street: Bakhtin's Anti-Linguistics." *Critical Inquiry* (December 1983), 265–81.

Streek, Jürgen. "Speech Acts in Interaction: A Critique of Searle." *Discourse Processes* 3 (1980), 133–53.

Stubbs, Michael. *Discourse Analysis: The Sociolinguistic Analysis of Natural Language.* Chicago: University of Chicago Press, 1983.

Sudnow, David, ed. *Studies in Social Interaction.* New York: Free Press, 1972.

Tannen, Deborah. "What's in a Frame? Surface Evidence for Underlying Expectations." In Roy Freedle ed., *New Dimensions in Discourse Processing.* Advances in Discourse Processes, vol. 2. Norwood, N.J.: Ablex, 1979, 137–81.

————. "New York Jewish Conversational Style." *International Journal of the Sociology of Language* 30 (1981), 133–39.

————. *Conversational Style: Analyzing Talk Among Friends.* Norwood, N.J.: Ablex, 1984.

Tedlock, Dennis. *Finding the Center: Narrative Poetry of the Zuni Indians.* Lincoln: University of Nebraska Press, 1978.

————. *The Spoken Word and the Work of Interpretation.* Philadelphia: University of Pennsylvania Press, 1983.

————. "Mayan Metasemiotics." In John Levitt and Bruce Mannheim, eds., *Vision and Interpretation,* forthcoming.

Trix, Frances. "What's in a Naming? Discourse Analysis Through Multiple Frames of an Islamic Lesson." Unpublished qualifying paper, Linguistics Department, University of Michigan, 1984.

————. "The Ashure Lament of Baba Rexheb and the Albanian Bektashi Community in America." In Alexander Popoviç, ed., *Bektashisme.* Paris: Centre Nationale de la Recherche Scientifique, 1992.

————. "Albanians in Michigan." In Arthur Hedvig, ed. *Building on Diversity: Ethnic Communities in Michigan.* Ann Arbor: University of Michigan Press, forthcoming.

————. "Bektashi Tekke and Sunni Mosque of Albanian Muslims in America." In Yvonne Haddad, and Jane Idleman Smith, eds., *Muslim Communities in the United States.* New York: Oxford University Press, forthcoming.

Trudgill, Peter. *On Dialect: Social and Geographical Perspectives.* New York: New York University Press, 1983.

————. *Dialects in Contact.* Oxford: Basil Blackwell, 1986.

Vaughan, Thomas. *A Grammar of the Turkish Language* (1709). Menston, England: Scolar Press, 1968.

Watzlawick, Paul, J. H. Beavin, and D. D. Jackson. *Pragmatics of Human Communication: A Study of Interactional Patterns, Pathologies, and Paradoxes.* New York: W. W. Norton, 1967.

Watzlawick, Paul, John Weakland, and Richard Fisch. *Change: Principles of Problem Formation and Problem Resolution.* New York: W. W. Norton, 1974.

Weinreich, Uriel. *Languages in Contact: Findings and Problems.* New York: Publications of New York Linguistic Circle no.1, 1953; reprint The Hague: Mouton, 1968.

————. "Is Structural Dialectology Possible?" (1954). In Harold Allen and Michael D. Linn, eds, *Dialect and Language Variation.* New York: Academic Press, 1986, 20–34.

Weinreich, Uriel, William Labov, and Maurice Herzog. "Empirical Foundations for a Theory of Language Change." In W. P. Lehmann and Yakov Malkiel, eds., *Directions for Historical Linguistics*. Austin: University of Texas Press, 1968.

Williams, Raymond. "Language." In *Marxism and Literature*. London: Oxford University Press, 1977.

Wodak, Ruth. "Discourse Analysis and Courtroom Interaction." *Discourse Processes* 3 (1980), 369–80.

Index

CONDUCT AND COMMUNICATION SERIES

Charles L. Briggs. *Competence in Performance: The Creativity of Tradition in Mexicano Verbal Art.* 1988.

Joseph J. Errington. *Structure and Style in Javanese: A Semiotic View of Linguistic Etiquette.* 1988.

Steven Feld. *Sound and Sentiment: Birds, Weeping, Poetics, and Song in Kaluli Expression.* Second edition. 1990.

Erving Goffman. *Forms of Talk.* 1981.

Erving Goffman. *Strategic Interaction.* 1970.

Dell Hymes. *Foundations in Sociolinguistics: An Ethnographic Approach.* 1974.

Dell Hymes. *"In vain I tried to tell you": Essays in Native American Ethnopoetics.* 1981.

Barbara Kirshenblatt-Gimblett, ed. *Speech Play: Research and Resources for the Study of Linguistic Creativity.* 1976.

Joel C. Kuipers. *Power in Performance: The Creation of Textual Authority in Weyewa Ritual Speech.* 1990.

William Labov. *Language in the Inner City: Studies in the Black English Vernacular.* 1973.

William Labov. *Sociolinguistic Patterns.* 1973.

Michael Moerman. *Talking Culture: Ethnography and Conversation Analysis.* 1987.

Dan Rose. *Black American Street Life: South Philadelphia, 1969–1971.* 1987.

Gillian Sankoff. *The Social Life of Language.* 1980.

Dennis Tedlock. *The Spoken Word and the Work of Interpretation.* 1983.

Frances Trix. *Spiritual Discourse: Learning with an Islamic Master.* 1992.

This book has been set in Linotron Galliard. Galliard was designed for Mergenthaler in 1978 by Matthew Carter. Galliard retains many of the features of a sixteenth-century typeface cut by Robert Granjon but has some modifications that give it a more contemporary look.

Printed on acid-free paper.